ART
BY COMMITTEE

A GUIDE TO ADVANCED
IMPROVISATION

"CHARNA AND DEL'S WORK AT IMPROVOLYMPIC MADE SENSE TO US AS
AN ART FORM AND FOR A POSITIVE OUTLOOK ON LIFE."
—TINA FEY

"DEL AND CHARNA GAVE ME A VISION. I DON'T KNOW
WHERE I'D BE WITHOUT THEM."
— AMY POEHLER

Book includes DVD with live
performances and interviews
with celebrity improv artists

CHARNA
HALPERN

MERIWETHER PUBLISHING LTD.
Colorado Springs, Colorado

Meriwether Publishing Ltd., Publisher
PO Box 7710
Colorado Springs, CO 80933-7710

www.meriwether.com

Editor: Arthur L. Zapel
Assistant editor: Audrey Scheck
Cover design: Scott Anderson, © 2005 The 5659 Design Co. 773-685-7019
Interview excerpts from i.O. 25th anniversary show courtesy of Kurtis
Productions, Chicago, Illinois.

Library of Congress Cataloging-in-Publication Data

Halpern, Charna, 1952-
    Art by committee : a guide to advanced improvisation / by Charna Halpern.
        p. cm.
    ISBN 978-1-56608-112-2 (pbk.)
    1. Improvisation (Acting) I. Title.
    PN2071.I5H25 2006
    792.02'8--dc22

                                                        2005035044

3   4   5   13   14   15

Dedication

Since the last time I wrote, my partner, the Guru … the mad scientist … Del Close, died.

On the morning of March 4th, Del requested the morphine drip that he was promised to make his last hours more comfortable. He was told that should he begin the morphine drip, he would fall asleep and never wake up. He had decided he was ready.

I sat on his bed and held his hand while we waited for the technician to bring the drip to the room. "Promise me you'll make the skull thing happen — no matter what," he said.

"I will," I promised.

"And keep my ashes in The Del Close Theater where I can affect the work."

"I will," I promised.

"And tell them all that we succeeded where others have failed. We created 'theater of the heart' — a theater where people cherish each other to succeed on-stage. Tell the students — 'theater of the heart.'" I began to cry at the beauty of what he had said. He was in great pain in his final hour, but still he concentrated on the importance of our work together. I witnessed absolutely no fear in him while he faced death, though I was shaking.

The technician arrived with the doctor and they put the morphine drip into his arm. "Turn it up!" he yelled in his booming voice. The doctor was a bit surprised, as Del had previously had two morphine shots that had taken no effect on him. The doctor turned it up, stating that she was still within the legal limits. A few seconds later, Del complained, "Come on — I used to be a drug addict. I know what I'm supposed to be feeling. Turn it up." The doctor turned it up again, stating that she was still within the legal limits. A few seconds later, Del's voice boomed again. "Turn it up!" "Jesus," the doctor said while turning it up again. "He's had enough to put out a horse." After a few seconds, Del sighed. As he closed his eyes for the last time, he spoke his last words, "Finally. I'm tired of being the funniest person in the room."

This book is dedicated to him.

"In the hands of a great master, all material is productive.
He can find a use for everything and everyone. He wastes nothing; therefore, he
always has enough. He values everyone: therefore, everyone values him."

—Wu Wei

"If we treat each other as if we are geniuses, poets, and artists, we have a better
chance of becoming that on-stage."

—Del Close

Table of Contents

Acknowledgments

Brian Stack, I cannot thank you enough for Del's interview and for the inspiration for this book.

I also send thanks and buckets of love to all of my alumni who are quoted in this book and who are, in turn, passing down pearls of wisdom to future performers. Thank you Adam McKay, Amy Poehler, Andy Dick, Rachel Dratch, Andy Richter, Neil Flynn, Mike Myers, Tim Meadows, Tina Fey, Susan Messing, Pete Hulne, Miles Stroth, Stephnie Weir, Dave Koechner, Kevin Dorff, Christina Gausas, and Dave Pasquesi.

Thanks to Rick Rios of Subliminal Films for his work on the DVD.

Thanks to Peter Gwinn who collaborated with me on *The Tag Out Performance Piece* on pages 26-29. I highly recommend his book, *Group Improvisation,* ISBN 978-1-56608-138-2.

A huge thank you to Mike Click for your critical eye, valuable help, and for taking up the slack at i.O. because I was too preoccupied writing this book. You are very important to me.

A special thanks to Scott Anderson who is always right by my side whenever I need an artistic genius to design something. Whether it is the marquee on my theater or the cover of my book – he is there to save the day.

I am very grateful to have Art Zapel as my publisher and friend. In my eyes, he is a king among men.

Last but not least, thanks to all of the i.O. performers who love and support our theater and help to pass down the torch to our new talent.

Foreword

Adam McKay

Writing the foreword to a book on improv is a bit of a contradiction. Improv is fast and current and defies categorization while the very mention of a foreword evokes dusty subterranean libraries and books on the Crimean War. So in an attempt to infuse some of the magic of improv into this foreword, I'm going to let myself free-form on the keyboard of my computer for the next thirty seconds. Whatever comes out is what goes in. I swear it. I've just gotten up and gotten a stop watch. So I'm ready. Here we go:

ghdflksdl;ippo … dog … a dog and a hat … uhhhh … Oh my God I regret this … This is awful … And it'll be in print … gotta think … Uhhhh … Jamaican Bobsled team!! … That is so weak … so weak … uhhhh … and time!

Okay. So that was something I tried. Hopefully in reading this book you can quickly do better improv than that. Now on with the foreword …

As a former student of Del and Charna's, I owe them and this work much. It, and they, literally re-taught me how to be creative. The basic lessons and ideas that Close developed through his lifetime and that Halpern continues to teach not only produce dynamic and electric improvised group performance pieces but also give students the basic fundamentals necessary to approach being a writer, actor, director, senator, optometrist, police sniper, etc. These are the essential and age-old tools of agreement and navigation that allow a person to treat obstacles, mistakes, difficult personalities, and insecurities as gifts and truths rather than reasons to fall back into clichés or fail. Del's entire mission was to generate relevant and honest work. The only failure was someone not participating in this goal.

In 1990 when I first took a class with Del on long-form improvisation, I remember being shell-shocked. Myself and five or six other improvisers were lucky enough to have Del treat us as his experimental ensemble. We developed new scenic improv forms, did the first all long-form show featuring one group and started another sketch group on the side called The Upright Citizen's Brigade.

But when I moved on to writing for television and film and then to directing, I was amazed at how well all of the tenets of Del's teaching held up. Agreement, focus, and finding your third and most original thought are ideas that translate to all disciplines. I don't always nail them, but they keep me in the ballpark.

In fact, after writing about the work they do and how great it is I'm starting to feel kind of cocky. I think I can do the thirty second improv writing thing. Screw it ... Here goes:

bah, dee, dah ... uhhh ... this is immediately not going well ... damn ... why am I sweating so much? ... Ahhhh ... Stop!

Okay. Once again that was a mistake.

Just read the book. It's that simple. But more importantly, use it. Perform and rehearse this work. Fail a lot and be proud of it. Read other books and take classes. And then if you're by chance in Chicago, go take a class at the i.O. Theater. And even if you're in Denver or Costa Rica, still take classes and start theater groups. Del's whole idea was to create a theater that can exist on its own, independent of corporate-owned TV and movies. This was supposed to be so special that when you filmed it, it was lost. Del wanted people playing up to their audiences, not down. He wanted entertainment that pushed us forward, not backwards or into a stasis.

He also used to say that by even showing up for class we were stepping away from the pack and becoming just a little bit special. It was a great thing to tell a class. It made us feel like we had a responsibility. Well, I think to a degree that's true of you opening up this book (Unless you're reading it while crouched in the aisle of the bookstore; either make a purchase or move on, you dirtbag). It's a choice that immediately separates you from the pack. So go and do amazing things. And if all else fails, just be honest.

— Adam McKay, 2005

4

Preface

At the end of my level one class, I love to hold a brief discussion with the students to see what questions they have about what they have learned so far. One of the things I am most often asked is, "What is the most important thing we should take with us on to level two?" It's then I must stress that the most important elements that they have learned in my class are not just the basics for level one but are the most important elements for doing the work, period. "The beginning is in the end," to quote Mike Myers from his introduction to my previous book, means just that. What we learn to do in the beginning is what we need to do in the end.

The basic concepts I teach are agreement and the ability to listen, remember, and recycle each other's ideas. I discuss these basics in depth in my seminal book, *Truth in Comedy*, which truly has become the bible for improvisation. I don't feel that it would be fair to readers to repeat myself from the past book, but I do need to refer to it from time to time, as all the work stems from the elements I wrote about before.

This new book is divided into three parts. Part One shows how some of our techniques have led to the creation of new forms. Part Two deals with helpful hints to further the advanced improviser. Part Three provides a bit of history on how the creators of long-form improvisation came together, along with some funny stories about Del Close which have so often been requested of me.

To get the most out of *Art by Committee*, I suggest having a copy of *Truth in Comedy* at your fingertips to refer to as well as a DVD player. This can be an incredible learning experience for you.

In the next few chapters, we will look at some of the best improvisers in the world. You will see the very skills that I teach in Part One being used by performers who, like neurosurgeons, wire brains together. You will see the power of connections and callbacks — the basics of all our work.

5

Introduction: Interview with Del Close

Del Close

Last year, when I began to write this book, I had no idea what the title would be, but I had some ideas of what I wanted it to contain. It was then that I received a gift in the mail from my friend Brian Stack, who is now writing for *Late Night with Conan O'Brien*. When Brian first began working with Del Close and me in the late '80s, he taped an interview with Del. He had recently come across it and decided that I might find use for it. Talk about serendipity! The interview was about Del's concept of "art by committee." I had found my title. The interview was so interesting that I transcribed it so that my readers can read Del's exact thoughts. The segment headings were written by Brian Stack. For those of you who never studied with Del … Ladies and Gentleman, in his own words, Del Close:

Harold Was Born out of Necessity

Harold began as a way to get all of the professional improvisers in The Committee on-stage improvising all at the same time. I've had a lot of improvising companies before. I took over The Committee in 1967 — summer of love — with Charlie Manson just down the street.

Everybody's hair was very long, everybody was sharing, everyone was doing everything in large groups. Sex, theater, politics; the whole thing — big bunches of people. My idea with the improvising company was to get the whole group of people out there and find some form or structure where everyone could play at the same time. Not just one person doing a monolog or three people doing a scene that they had been improvising and re-improvising — basically rehearsing a show in front of an audience that they had been preparing for weeks. I wanted to do a show where we could create *art by committee*. I really hate it when I run into someone who says, "Well, you can't think as well as a group as you can as an individual. Art is an individual undertaking, so you might as well not even try."

No! Art is possible by committee. Basically all you need is some structure, traffic patterns, game rules, and some kind of image of what it is you want to do. And it turned out to be Harold.

It's so complex, and you have to pay so much attention and entertain the audience with jokes at the same time — it's almost a fruitless undertaking. What the audience laughs at — and indeed will cheer at — are the moments of discovery — moments of connection — where the art by committee — where the group brain — really does start functioning. We see amazing kinds of communication going on between people. I've done this, of course, myself. Otherwise I wouldn't have gotten hooked on it.

Harold Performers Have a Unique Relationship with One Another

Nothing that we say to each other is innocent of emotional manipulation. Everything we do on-stage is to affect each other in some way, and if we notice very carefully how those "swine" we are working with are trying to get to us and at us ... sometimes I suggest that we perform on-stage as if we are a whole bunch of raving paranoids. Nothing that I hear is going to be simple. Nothing that you say to me is going to be accepted at face value. *Ooooh* — we always mean something else.

(See *Truth in Comedy* for further explanation of this idea.)

Rather Than Mold Everyone the Same Way, Del Prefers It When the Improviser Grows As an Individual — However Unusual He or She May Be

We get some real oddballs in this work. And I think we develop our own peculiarities. Rather than become the ideal Harold performer, we need to develop our own peculiarities.

Unlike at Second City where Del Spent Many Hilarious Years, the Harold at i.O. (formerly ImprovOlympic) Consists of People Acting Like Themselves Most of the Time

We hardly ever play characters. But we realize perfectly well that all the characters that we play are really subsets of ourselves. It's ourselves in slightly different moods — ourselves carrying a little more emotional freight. Back to how important emotions are: the small ones — the teensiest, weensiest emotional discovery that's real — beats the hell out of the biggest one that's phony. And that's why our audience, I think, is so much on our side. They want us to succeed. They're cheering us on. They see us doing something while making a hip discovery. It's like they're giving us body English: "Go, go, make it, make it!" They are definitely on your side. It's not an antagonistic relationship with the audience like with a comedian trying to make the audience laugh. No. We're going to do something in the presence of the audience. It's like an inductive thing. We draw them along with it.

Just Like Musicians Learn from Other Musicians, Del Learned from Watching Many Great Improvisers

Most of the things we lay on you were not invented; they were observed. I saw the best improvisers in the country working for many years. What were they doing? Well, I'm not bad in the analysis department. I would analyze it, figure it out, and do it myself.

Exercises based on Del's interview

I dealt with the idea of listening for the game in a scene and being affected by each others' initiations in *Truth in Comedy*. After hearing Del say in his interview that he often thought we should pretend to be paranoid psychotics on-stage, I thought these class exercises would be fun to include.

Exercise One: The Paranoid Psychotic

(Two Players)

I instruct my students to listen to every line and pretend they are paranoid before they respond. I ask them to repeat the line spoken to them and heighten the word or words that displayed the deeper hidden meaning. I ask for a paranoid response. The second player is to react in the same way.

Example:

PLAYER 1: You look nice today.

PLAYER 2: *(Thinking and reacting in a paranoid manner first)* I look nice *today*. What is that supposed to mean? I look bad on other days, but today I look good? I guess I shouldn't be upset if *you're* giving me a compliment.

PLAYER 1: If *I'm* giving you a compliment? Do you think I'm negative? I give compliments. *I* am not a negative person.

PLAYER 2: Are you saying *I'm* negative? I am not negative. I am a positive person. I am friendly. I have charisma.

PLAYER 1: *You think I don't have charisma?* I do. I have

charisma. And fashion sense. I look good today, don't I? *(By now, the players should be raging mad.)*

I am not suggesting all scenes should be played this way by any means. It would be quite annoying. But it is a great exercise for students to practice slowing down before they respond to a line. They will try to dig deeper to find more meaning in the line spoken to them. They will get the idea that there is greater meaning in the line spoken to them than what is actually said.

Exercise Two: Psychotic Rants
(Two Players)

There is another exercise that I have recently added to our curriculum that was given to me by Christina Gausas, one of our leading performers and teachers. This exercise also depends on us going off the deep end a bit. But it is so cathartic. Mainly, it teaches us to break through the part of our brain that thinks we can go no further. It also helps to get a performer to crank up the emotions if he or she is having trouble doing so.

One player gives a banal line to the other. That first player will do nothing more for the rest of the exercise. The lesson of the exercise is for the second player. The second player listens to the first player's line and slowly reacts and builds into what will be a screaming, raving rant. This should go on until a blood vessel is about to burst or the player practically blacks out on-stage. He cannot stop unless it's to take a breath. He must keep going. He cannot stop to think. This is important because we want the player to lose control so that just when he thinks he can't think of anything else to say, he will break through, and more ideas will flow.

Example:

PLAYER 1: I'm sorry, sir. We are out of bananas.

PLAYER 2: Out of bananas? My girlfriend sent me out to buy bananas, and I have to go back to her empty-handed!!! One little task — get bananas — and I fail!! What kind of a man am I? I can't even provide for my girlfriend. She will

11

never marry me now. I will be alone forever … you might as well castrate me … I'm not a man … I am nothing … *(On and on and on.)*

It's fun to hear the information the players can come up with when demonstrating psychotic behavior and even more fun to see just how far they can go.

Part 1
i.O. Forms:
Art by Committee

CHAPTER 1:
The New Harold

Since my last book, there have been many developments in the work. The Harold described in my first book is incredible training for our work. The Harold has been transforming, but it's still based on the same principles that made the original Harold. The work has become sophisticated and beautiful. I had many requests to write another book, but I was stymied. How would I describe the type of work that's now going on at i.O? How does one describe a beautiful painting and do it justice? How does one describe a magnificent dance? How could I describe the magic that appears on my stage? The task seemed daunting to me ... mind-numbing. Finally, I discovered the answer: a DVD.

As you will recall, the Harold I wrote about before had the structure of an opening and three scenes that would return in spans of time with games and monologs interspersed throughout. Del always told me that this was to be the "training wheels" Harold. He said the work would eventually transform using the main principles. It's like learning the notes to the musical scale — you don't have to sing the same song all the time. In that spirit, our work on the Harold is still based on remembering everything and wasting nothing while weaving together unrelated scenes that soon come to be a non-linear story. Oh, thank God for DVDs.

Over the years, I have been blessed to have some of the most amazing performers grace my stage. I've seen the magical Harold appear with teams like Baron's Barracudas, Blue Velveeta, The Family, and People of Earth. One of my favorites was The Family. This was a group of six men who are pictured in my previous book. The team had total trust and support and never stopped to judge one another or think

15

about the direction the piece was going to take. They trusted one another to follow and use everything. The work was always brilliant. Del said that watching The Family was like watching six men fall down the stairs at the same time and land on their feet. That is the secret of this work. It gets out of control. You follow it. It leads you. However, the players do have an awareness on-stage that Miles Stroth, a member of The Family, refers to as *playing the piece rather than the scene* ... You start with scenes but once a few scenes have happened, a show is being created. You start opening your awareness. I'm not only aware of the scenes I am in, but how they connect to one another and what pattern they're creating. I start thinking, 'how can I best fill in the rest of this show?' I start playing the piece."

The Importance of the Opening

I have always believed that the opening is the most important part of the Harold. In my first book I discussed how the first level of connections occurs when the first beat of scenes comes out of the information from the opening. I compared the opening of the Harold to the importance of a good foundation when building a house. You can't start building a house from the roof down. Another reason the opening is so important is that it gives the group the opportunity to develop its point of view. This is the start of developing what is known as **The Group Mind**. After a good opening, the team will know what their piece is going to be about and the thesis statement they are setting out to prove. If you have a strong opening, you are not entering into a Harold blindly. The themes that the teams set out to explore return again and again throughout the piece and usually return at the end to tie everything up in a nice, neat little package.

Levels of Meaning

Del always taught us to take the suggestion, no matter how banal, and investigate the potential for deeper meaning.

16

Raise the level of the suggestion. This is why there is no such thing as a bad suggestion. We have the power to elevate it to provide the audience with a religious experience. If we really explore the suggestion at the top of our intelligence it will be compelling. It isn't about "wet cardboard," it's about the meaning of life. The suggestion should not be taken literally. This is how we get levels of meaning in our work. One of my groups received "the solar system" as a suggestion for their Harold. The first player came to the center of the stage and slowly began twirling as he slowly repeated the phrase, "I am the center of the universe." Another player began revolving around him, slowly singing the words, "Me me me me me me me me." A third player also began to revolve around the center player and repeatedly sang his verse, "My world revolves around you." The fourth player shot past the others from one corner of the stage to the opposite corner of the stage, pretending to be a comet, while singing at a faster rate, "got no time for you, got no time for you." All these improvised simple tunes began to blend melodically and contrapuntally. The others on-stage added to the physical initiation of creating a solar system. While the players were inspired by the suggestion on one level and created a physical solar system, they found the meaning of their piece on another level, which was solipsism, selfishness, and even a bit of stalking.

In short, if you are given the suggestion of jumping jacks, refrain from the impulse of doing five minutes of jumping jacks on-stage. We know what jumping jacks are, and we know that you know what they are. You don't have to show us. Your job is to take that suggestion and discover a theme for the piece.

The Basic Building Blocks of the Harold

The Harold consists of many things: scenes, songs, games, and monologs. But the most important of these things is the two-person scene. We need strong scenes so that we have strong stories to follow and weave together in the piece.

Basically, a scene consists of a strong, genuine relationship

17

between the two main characters that we can explore throughout the piece. It is through this relationship that their past is revealed. The characters should be as three-dimensional as possible, with real emotions. We need to see why they feel as they do and why they change (and sometimes someone has to change for the scene to succeed). I tell my students to always start in a realistic situation and let us see how things may get out of hand later on. I recently read a critic's review of a new comedy show for television. The critic said, "I didn't laugh because the situations were relentlessly awkward and left no room for actual character development or buyable dialogue." Our job here is to try to bring real slices of life to the stage.

That's not to say that we shouldn't make unusual choices. One of my favorite scenes was written by Del Close and some of the Baron's Barracudas in a review we produced here at i.O. called "Honor Finegan vs. The Brain of the Galaxy." The scene was a serial killer's support group. The characters were all the serial killers you've ever read about – Charlie Manson, David Berkowitz, John Wayne Gacy, Charles Starkweather, and the list goes on. The actors richly mined these characters and played them as normally as possible with sincere reasons for what they did. The hilarity comes in the normalcy of this support group. Starkweather says that killing was something he liked, something he was good at. "Is it wrong to do something you're good at?" All the characters agree in support. When Starkweather worries that people will think he was crazy and that "no one remembers a crazy person," his fellow serial killers feel instant sympathy and give him a group hug. This was a funny scene because we were seeing these unusual people reacting in much the same way any other person would act in a support group. Universal truths elicit laughs.

We have all heard by now that the important elements of a scene are the who, what, and where; who we are to each other, where we are, and what is going on between us. These are all things that need to be discovered in your scene. We will be dealing with character through environment a little later on in this book. As to finding the relationship, I always give away this little secret in my classes. You will find your relationship in the

18

first three lines of your scene. Pay close attention to those lines — it's always there.

Follow the Focus of the Scene

I want to reiterate that while the Harold may be more sophisticated and we are no longer being slaves to the form, the principles that make this work successful should not be forgotten. The most important idea of the Harold is that we are following the relationships of characters in three different storylines (Del used to jokingly compare the Harold form to the old TV show, *The Love Boat*). A mistake that I see troupes make most often is they do not follow the focus of the first scene. For example, one night I watched a Harold, and one of the first scenes in the first beat of the Harold was a wonderful scene about a man placing a bet at the race track. His wife caught him and begged him to stop gambling the family's money away. She threatened to leave him if he didn't stop. He begged her to let him place one more bet. It was a sure thing. He was clearly addicted to gambling. The race was run, and he lost. This scene was a great start. Then the piece went south because the second beat of that scene took place at the stable where the jockey was grooming the horse while talking to the owner of the horse. They were starting a whole new scene. If they were paying attention to the focus of the first scene, we would be following the original couple. Did the man have to tell his son that he gambled away the son's tuition to school, perhaps? Did the wife and child leave the man? These are the things that need to be followed in this story line. When the players forget the focus of the scene and begin new relationships in every beat, the Harold tends to peter out at the end. We must not forget Del's vision. We need these three separate story lines to weave together and connect at the end. Follow the relationships you have created in the beginning. You don't have time to keep creating new relationships in every beat. We want to get to know these people. You have a story to tell. Follow through on the story of the gambler; it's not about the owner of the horse. Del once quoted a Zen Buddhist saying when discussing the focus of the scene: "Finger points to moon; do not confuse finger with moon."

I have chosen to show you a team that has taken the work even further. They are called The Reckoning. They have the same qualities that I mentioned, but they have added another dimension to the work. Many of the main ideas of their pieces are discovered through their edits. An edit in the past has been a simple crossover of the previous scene which lets the players from the last scene know that they may leave the stage in order for the new scene to begin. But with The Reckoning everything is part of the piece; everything is beautiful. Their edit is a transformation of a previous idea that later becomes part of the story. It is wonderful to watch because, clearly, they have no idea why they are doing what they do — but not one player hesitates to follow what another person initiates. There is no judgment whatsoever. Something is created and later used. "The Master wastes nothing." The viewer gets that same feeling Del talked about when describing The Family. They are on a roller coaster — out of control. Yet it all comes together beautifully, and the audience is brought to its feet cheering. The audience is then made to think that the performers were in control the whole time.

This is why we preach trust, support, and the ultimate love for one another. It's not just because we would like to make you better people (although that does come with the territory.) It's because that is how the work will be truly successful. Observe, when watching the DVD, how one player will do a movement that seems perplexing or initiate a silly sound. The team does not stop to say, "What the hell is that?" They cherish the initiation. It now belongs to them. It is made into something that will be remembered and become vital to the piece later on. They trust one another to take care of their ideas and make one another look good. They trust one another on a physical level as well, whether they are flying someone around the stage, as they do in the show you are about to watch, or catching someone as they fall from the top of an imaginary building, which I've seen them do in the past.

I have seen people take flying leaps of faith by running across the stage and jumping into each other's arms. Though it is what I preach, it still amazes me when it happens. I remember talking to Del about the incredible level of trust we see on our stage. I asked him, "What is it exactly that makes these people take flying leaps into each other's arms?" Del replied, "I don't know, but it must be the same thing that makes those other people catch them."

When watching The Reckoning, notice the patterns in the opening and the way they play with the issues of the legal aspects of organ donors as well as gay rights. All of this is discovered through their suggestion of surgery.

Watch "The Reckoning" Sequence on the DVD

Del's General Principles for the Harold

1. You are all supporting actors.
2. Always check your impulses.
3. Never enter a scene unless you are *needed!*
4. Save your fellow actor, don't worry about the piece.
5. Your prime responsibility is to support.
6. Work at the top of your brains at all times.
7. Never underestimate or condescend to your audience.
8. No jokes (unless it is tipped in front that it is a joke).
9. Trust ... trust your fellow actors to support you:
   a. Trust them to come through if you lay something heavy on them.
   b. Trust yourself.
10. Avoid judging what is going down except in terms of whether it needs help (either by entering or cutting), what can best follow, or how you can support imaginatively if your support is called for.
11. *Listen!*

CHAPTER 2:
The Tag Out Performance Piece

i.O. is famous for teaching long-form improvisation, so, naturally, when new students start their classes they are eager to jump in and try their hands at it. Of course, long-form is very difficult without first learning the basic principles of agreement, building on one another's ideas, and bringing scenes back in different spans of time. So, to help my students learn these lessons quickly, I developed an exercise that only succeeds when these principles are followed. I love doing this in the beginning classes because then the new students go right past the mistakes usually made in a beginning improvisation class. The piece is based on a technique we use in our Harolds called a **tag out**.

How a Tag Out Is Used

A Harold starts off with three different improvised scenes. Over the course of the Harold, each of these scenes will return, showing the relationship of the characters at different points in time. The scenes will connect and weave together. The tag out can be used to help heighten and explore an individual relationship or scene, and it can help connect different scenes together.

Here's an example of how the tag out can be used to heighten an individual scene:

Two players start by improvising a scene between a father and son. In the scene, the father is accusing the son of doing drugs. He says to his son, "I'm going to find out who's been giving you drugs if I have to go to every person in this city!"

A third actor taps the son on the shoulder and takes his place on-stage, thus *tagging him out*. The new actor says,

"Well Wilson, I let the boys come next door to play basketball, but I certainly don't give them drugs!"

A fourth actor tags out the next door neighbor and says, "Well, Mr. Wilson, as principal of Hill High School, I assure you there are no drug problems here!"

A fifth actor tags out the principal and says, "I sell to a lot of kids. How do I know which one is yours?" The father shows him a picture. "Oh yeah, I know your kid," the dealer says.

Finally, the actor who played the son tags out the drug dealer and says, "OK, you caught me," and the scene continues on from there. Using the tag out, we have sent the father all around the city in a matter of seconds!

You should notice a few things about how the tag out works before I go on. First of all, when a tag out is used, the actor who is not tagged out always remains the same character so that there is no confusion about what's being heightened. Second, when a tag out is used, it always indicates a jump in time and space. In other words, the scene following the tag out shows the character who is not tagged out in a different place talking to a different person.

A good tag out is based on a strong one-line initiation (which is another reason I teach it to beginning classes). We should know from a character's first line who he is and what new information he is bringing to the table.

If this were part of a Harold, the neighbor, principal, and drug dealer would probably never be seen again, as they were created just to heighten one idea. However, when a tag out is used to connect scenes together, we may see characters that already exist.

Here's an example of how the tag out can be used to connect scenes together:

Two players improvise a scene in which a manager is interviewing a woman in his office for a job at McDonald's. He tells her, "Working the grill is a big responsibility, so you must be reliable. The last employee I had at the grill wasn't as careful as he needed to be, so I had to fire him."

At this point the actor who played the son in our previous example now tags out the woman. He returns as the drug-crazed son, this time working the grill, messing up, and perhaps setting himself on fire. The manager realizes that he is no longer in his office but at the grill, catches the son messing up, and fires him. The woman then tags out the son again and returns to the job interview. The scene continues, and both the father-son scene and the manager-employee scene have been furthered by new information.

A tag out doesn't always have to end with a return to the original scene. For example, a third player could tag out the manager after he fires the son and initiate a scene between the son and one of his friends by saying, "Don't feel bad, dude. I got fired from Wendy's for drinking Frosties straight out of the machine." Then their scene could continue, as we learn what the son does with his friends at night. However, you will find that it is usually very satisfying to eventually return to the original scene.

A third way the tag out can be used is to show the truth about what really happened in some situation. An example would be a woman asking her boyfriend why he stood her up for their date the night before. He tells her that he was so exhausted from studying all day for the Bar Exam that he fell asleep. A second woman tags out the girlfriend and begins making out with the boy. The girlfriend quickly tags out the second woman and continues the scene with, "Well, I guess I can't get mad if you were studying so hard." The second woman made the boyfriend a liar with a quick tag out.

It is important to note that some tag outs are very quick, as in the previous example. After actors are tagged out, they must stay on their toes so that they can come back into the piece at the right time. This also means that the actors must stay in tune with one another to decide whether to let the run of tag outs continue for a while or to return to the previous scene immediately.

Using this tag out idea, I created a form to not only teach tag outs but also to reinforce the idea of scenes returning in spans of time.

The Tag Out Performance Piece

In this piece, a story is created entirely by tag outs. A tag out is the only way to enter the piece. Usually, each actor will only play one character throughout the piece. The actors need to stay on their toes and be ready to return often at any time. When characters return, it will rarely be in a place or time that we've seen them before. This is not a linear piece.

For a suggestion, I usually ask for a line of poetry. This suggestion is just something to "let hang in the air." It is not the opening line, nor is it the theme of the first scene. It's just an idea to inspire us as a group and affect the piece overall.

The first scene begins with two characters. This scene should be allowed to go on for awhile, because the more information the scene generates, the more ideas the other players will have to build the story. A third player will edit the first scene by tagging out one of the players. From that point on, everyone will need to stay on their toes, listening carefully and looking for ways to build on the ideas that the group has created.

Here is an example of how a tag out piece might go:

Scene 1
(Doug and Karen play a man walking a woman home after their first date. After a while:)
KAREN: Well, tonight was … interesting. I thought I would hate greyhound racing. And I was right.
DOUG: It's still early. Let's go get a drink.
KAREN: No thanks, I'm really tired.
DOUG: Hey, that dinner was expensive. At least we could make out for awhile. *(BOB tags out KAREN.)*

Scene 2
BOB: Wow. She actually punched you in the face?
DOUG: I never saw it coming. That girl was crazy!
BOB: You know, none of my other roommates ever get beat up on dates. Maybe it's you.
DOUG: What? No way. I'm a perfect gentleman. *(MARY tags out BOB.)*

Scene 3
MARY: How dare you insult my weight like that!
DOUG: Hey, sorry! I thought you were pregnant! *(MARY slaps DOUG, ALEXANDRA tags out MARY.)*

Scene 4
ALEXANDRA: You Pig!
DOUG: What? I'm just saying that chick was hot! *(ALEXANDRA slaps DOUG, REBECCA tags out ALEXANDRA.)*

Scene 5
DOUG: Can you pay for this? *(REBECCA slaps DOUG, KIM tags out REBECCA.)*

Scene 6
(KIM slaps DOUG.)
DOUG: I didn't even say anything yet! *(BOB tags out KIM.)*

Back to Scene 2
DOUG: Do you really think it's me?
BOB: You gotta learn how to treat women right. You gotta talk nice to them and give flowers. Tell them they're pretty and that you like to cook. That's what women want. *(STUART tags out BOB.)*

Scene 7
STUART: Well, Doug, your mother liked me because I was a fireman. Women love firemen. You should treat a woman like you're saving her from a burning building. *(KIM tags out STUART.)*

Back to Scene 6
(KIM slaps DOUG. STUART tags out KIM.)

Back to Scene 7
STUART: Like the building's on fire, not like she's on fire!
DOUG: So I shouldn't have made her stop, drop, and roll? *(NICK tags out STUART.)*

Scene 8
NICK: Doug, my man, you listen to ol' Stubby Fingers Magee. Lovin' a woman is just like playin' the saxophone. You gotta be gentle, hit all the right notes, and listen to the music that she's makin'. *(BILL tags out DOUG.)*

Scene 9
BILL: Stubby fingers Magee, you listen to ol' blind Lemon Samuels. Playing the saxophone is just like lovin' a woman. You got to be gentle ... *(REBECCA tags out NICK.)*

Scene 10
REBECCA: We've got good news, Mr Samuels. Your tests have come back, and you will regain your sight. You're not blind.
BILL: Oh doctor, this is terrible! I can't be a famous jazz musician if I'm not blind! *(The scene continues for awhile between BLIND LEMON and his DOCTOR. MARY tags out BILL.)*

Scene 11 *(connects to Scene 3)*
MARY: Doctor, I think I might be pregnant ...

... and the piece continues, following the characters around and heightening the themes of love and respect, image versus reality, and any other themes that arise.

Let's take a look at some of the moves that our players made in this example.

Scene 1 would obviously be longer than the example to develop more themes and information for us to explore. This led us to Scene 2, where we jump in time to later that night, after the date. This allows us to leave the violence at the end of the date to the imagination of the audience.

In the middle of Scene 2, after Doug says that he's a perfect gentleman, we see a series of quick scenes (Scenes 3-6) showing that, in fact, he is not a gentleman. A quick series of scenes that heightens one idea is called a **run**. At the end of the run, we returned to Scene 2.

Later in the scene, we left on another run showing Doug

asking various people for advice. But during this run, the players decided not to return to Scene 2 and instead created a transition to another scene. Once we realize that we are expanding our world to find a new relationship, we have left the run and are now creating a **chain**. The chain (Scenes 8 and 9) takes us to Scene 10. Rebecca had appeared in the piece once before, as one of the unlucky dates. However, her appearance as the date was very short and functional. So Rebecca is free to enter as a different character.

When Mary appears in the doctor's office in Scene 11, she decides that she will play her character from Scene 3 in the earlier run. So Mary makes a connection: she has caused the chain of scenes to loop back around on itself.

Once the piece is underway, it's fine to add additional moves and break the rules a bit. If it is important for a character to join a scene without tagging anyone out, he may do so. Then, if another player wants to do a scene alone with the main character, he can just tag out two people instead of one. I have seen scenes where a group of people are in the piece, such as a classroom scene, and a person initiated a tag out just by waving the whole class away. Sometimes two actors may realize that the story demands that they do a scene together without any other characters. In that case, they can just walk on-stage in front of the previous scene and begin their own, signaling to the previous scene that they have been edited. These are the same editing techniques that we use in the Harold, as described in my book, *Truth in Comedy*.

Beer Shark Mice

A number of years ago, I received a call from Pete Hulne, who started with i.O. in Chicago in the mid-eighties and now is a successful actor in Los Angeles and still a member of my theater family at i.O. West. He said that he and other long-term i.O. family members Neil Flynn, David Koechner, Mike Coleman, and Pat Finn wanted to perform together and do something different. After all, they had mastered the Harold years ago, and it was time to create a new form for themselves. I described my tag out piece to Peter over the phone. He thought it was an interesting seed to begin with. Like all great improvisers, these pros were able to take an idea, run with it, and change it to make it their own. That's what makes working at i.O. so much

Beer Shark Mice. Left to Right: Mike Coleman, Pat Finn, Dave Koechner, Neil Flynn, and Pete Hulne.

fun. Someone can create something that inspires someone else to take that idea in a new direction. It keeps everyone on their toes. Everyone inspires one another to make something better, and the work is always changing.

Beer Shark Mice created a form that starts like a tag out. They have slightly changed the rules. For one thing they play many different characters. But the skills they use to create different worlds that collide together in the span of thirty to forty minutes are the very skills that I want to point out to you. These are the skills of a great improviser. I will soon direct you to the Beer Shark Mice section on your DVD and ask you to keep an eye out for specific things.

In *Truth in Comedy,* I discussed the importance of connections. I explained that this is truly the way to get laughs. You will see exactly what I mean when the simplest ideas are remembered and brought back into different scenes. Early in the piece, one of the players calls the ship a boat. He is admonished by the character in the scene with him. That smallest detail is not forgotten later in the piece. In *Truth in Comedy,* I discussed the importance of specifics. You will see how not one detail slips by these players. Pete Hulne accidentally sings the wrong words from a Jim Croce song. He sings, "If I could *spend* time in a bottle." Neil Flynn could not pass that up. Everything is heard. The actual words are, "If I could *save* time in a bottle." Neil points this out and this line, which is seemingly a mistake, is used later in the piece when the song writers are trying to write the words to the song. I have briefly discussed the idea of the importance of playing the mistakes in *Truth in Comedy*. Here you can see my point that mistakes are really discoveries. Play with them. They are "gold," as Neil Flynn said to me after the show. They become the best part of the show. That's why I always inform my beginning students that the only real mistake is to ignore the mistakes in their work. That's why these performers are so good. They hear everything and use it — especially the mistakes. *The master wastes nothing.*

Del used to talk about a phrase the French use called *esprit d' l'escalier*, which is translated to mean "spirit of the stairway." It refers to the moment when you find the correct answer, but it's already too late. For example, you are in a scene, and something happens that you don't handle well. When the scene is over and you are leaving the stage — or going down that magic stairway — the right answer pops into your head. But it's too late. The scene is over. That is why our work is so much fun. You do get to return to that scene and use that right answer or fix that mistake.

While watching Beer Shark Mice, pay close attention to the patterns created in the work, the mirror images of scenes brought back. You will be watching the best players at remembering and recycling one another's ideas.

Another important thing to note is the physical play that Pete Hulne and Pat Finn inspire in their team. These two are the best physical players I have ever seen. This entire team plays hard, as you will see. Too often I see talking heads on-stage and no physical play. It is so important to remember that you as an improviser create a whole new world for us, the audience, through your work in building the environment. The physical world is another level of laughs and is too often ignored. And as you can see, it can be sidesplitting to watch. Pay attention to their incredible level of commitment in every aspect of their play on-stage. It is also proof positive that when the performers are having fun on-stage, we are having even more fun watching.

Watch "Beer Shark Mice" Sequence on the DVD

CHAPTER 3:
Using Monologs in the Work

Since this book is for the advanced improviser, we will take the basics from book one further. The monolog game is used as an opening to a Harold in my first book. Personal monologs are a great source of inspiration in our openings and add texture throughout our work on-stage. As the monologist, it is a great opportunity to show oneself to the audience and display some vulnerability. And, again, that truthfulness that I am always yammering about reminds the audience that we share the same world. But what do the players do with that information? It's not enough to simply replay the monolog in the form of a scene. Why show us what we've just heard? The job of the improviser is to listen to the whole idea of that monolog and say something back to the monologist through the scene. Prove or disprove their theory, if you will. To do this, the player must transplant that idea into a different context altogether.

An example of the idea from the monolog being transplanted into a brief scene is from a show with The Family. In this scene, Neil Flynn came out to do a monolog on the Academy Awards. He talked about how he was sometimes disappointed with the outcome. For instance, he couldn't believe that Jack Lemmon won for *Save the Tiger*. At the end of Neil's monolog, Matt Besser asked in disbelief, "Neil, did you see that movie?" Neil sheepishly replied, "No, but I don't have to know about something to have an opinion." The team instantly edited him and jumped out for a scene.

(NEIL knocks on a door that is answered by MATT. TINA FEY is with MATT in the improvised home.)
NEIL: Excuse me. I'm collecting signatures to send Doug

Carlson to the Senate.

MATT: I hate Doug Carlson. Doug Carlson is *nothing*. *(He slams the door in NEIL's face, and NEIL shrugs and walks Off-stage.)*

TINA: *(to MATT)* Who's Doug Carlson?

MATT: I have no idea.

This scene clearly demonstrates Neil's thought and has inspired a scene for the players to use in another situation. Let's examine another monolog where the players find a way to let the monologist know they highly disagree with his point of view.

In class, a student told us in his monolog that he was recently married and that he loved married life. He and his wife had developed a routine and they follow that same routine every day. They wake up in the morning, he drives her to work, he picks her up, she makes dinner, he does the dishes, they read and go to bed. Day after day, it is the same routine. He loved the fact that he knew what he was going to be doing every single day. He just loved married life!

Two players jumped onto the stage and began a scene that took place in the military.

MAN 1: You know, the army really isn't so bad.

MAN 2: Nah. Getting up before dawn isn't as hard as I thought it would be.

MAN 1: And all this exercise isn't really too grueling.

MAN 2: And the food isn't that bad.

MAN 1: *(In tears)* I don't miss my girlfriend too much.

(Both men end the scene by sobbing on each other's shoulders.)

Clearly, the main idea that inspired the players was that the monologist was trying to make the best out of a bad situation. At least, that is how the players interpreted the monologist's words. They felt his life was like the military, and that he was in a rut. This inspired the monologist to come back and defend himself to the players and the play between the two was hilarious. At the end of the piece, he admitted that things were not great and that he was going to go home and have a talk with his wife. Mission accomplished! We ruined a marriage and saved a life.

The piece we are about to show on your DVD is from the longest-running show in Chicago and certainly one of the most important. It is called The Armando Diaz Theatrical Experience and Hootenanny. It is a show created on a monologist's point of view throughout the piece. A speaker leads the way and provides the inspiration to the players who, in turn, show him what they think after his statements are processed and filtered through their brains. And, like all of our work, there are scenic connections, ideas that take on new meaning each time they return, and lots of wonderful surprises.

Original cast of The Armando Diaz Theatrical Experience and Hootenanny.

The monologist in this show you are about to see is Joe Bill. I picked Joe because his monologs always come from a very emotional place. You will see how the players are able to use that emotion in their character work when being inspired by Joe's story. It is his vulnerability and honesty in sharing his life experiences that fuels the short piece.

In the previous section of the DVD, preceding Armando Diaz, I have included another example of a monologist providing inspiration to the players. The piece is from The Upright Citizens Brigade with Tina Fey and Amy Poehler performing at i.O.'s twentieth anniversary. You will see how the performers are able to create new stories while connecting to the ideas of the original monolog.

Watch the "Armando" (The Armando Diaz Theatrical Experience and Hootenanny) Sequence and the "Upright Citizens Brigade" Sequence on the DVD.

Part 2
The Improviser

CHAPTER 4:
What Makes an Improviser Good

The thing I love about improvisation is it gives the younger improvisers a reason to study if they are still in school and the older improvisers a reason to continue their education. I firmly believe, by the way, that improvisation should be mandatory for all college students, not only to enhance studying but to increase confidence and build self-esteem. One of my favorite moments on-stage was watching a team that I trained from Northwestern University. The students were from diverse backgrounds. Some were majoring in theater, others in science and engineering. In this particular show, the theme was "bonds." One of the students came out and did a monolog on "ionic bonding." It was hilarious, and he received a standing ovation. After the show he came up to me and said, "I never thought I'd find any use for that information." Everything you know, whether it be mathematics or cooking recipes, will find a place to turn up in your work. I have seen teams narrate mythological scenes in one beat and do political satire in the next. It's important to know what's going on in the world so that you, as a player, can reflect what the audience is feeling.

You must continue being a student of the world. You have a responsibility to say something to your audience on-stage. Remember, they are paying to see you, so you'd better know what has happened in the news that day and bone up on current events. I, for one, am an example of your typical audience member. Very recently I read a few articles in the paper that made me very paranoid. One story told about a new weapon the government has which will take the place of bullets. It's a laser that shoots at the speed of light. It cannot be dodged like a bullet. It can also shoot through walls. This is great news for the army and in a number of years will probably be reconfigured for police forces. We already have cameras in various parts of the city — not for privacy invasion, oh no, but for crime. O'Hare Airport has a touch screen where any portion of the airport can now be seen by the touch of a finger. Can something like this be developed on a larger scale for a whole city? Perhaps, someday. In my paranoid mind, we are facing a future where we can be found at any time and shot with lasers through the walls of our homes. While we are told these are developments to fight terrorists and criminals, I already know of a friend who received a ticket in the mail because a camera took a picture of her driving without a seat belt. And the city told her a picture of proof will not be given to her. She was just ordered to pay. That sounds to me like her constitutional rights have already gone out the window.

When I go to an improv show, I want the performers to talk to me about the issues that worry me. Either allay my fears or make me even more paranoid and tell me I'm not alone in my dark little world. Tim Meadows said that what he got most from our approach to comedy was cynicism and a lack of trust for authority. "I became more cynical — questioning politicians, media, relationships, and people. Not cynical in a bad way — cynical in a good way," he said. Read

T. J. Jagadowski (left) and Dave Pasquesi

the papers every day, watch the news, familiarize yourself with the classics, find your voice, and form an opinion. If you don't have anything to say, what is there to be funny about?

One of our biggest shows at the i.O. in Chicago is The T.J. and Dave Show, which features two of the most respected players in the improvisational community, T.J. Jagadowski and Dave Pasquesi. In their show, they have discussed everything from politics to philosophy to geometry while blowing people's minds. They bring an intelligence to their shows that works on many levels. We must have something to talk about besides "you stole my girlfriend," or "you didn't pay your share of the rent this month." Del always taught us to stay away from the trite and mundane. He wanted us, at best, to be interesting.

It is important to have a high reference level so that you are able to support the ideas of your fellow players. I remember a beautiful scene started in one of my classes on the suggestion of "forgiveness." Someone started the scene pretending to be Jesus on the cross. He looked at his fellow player and said, "Judas, I forgive you." His fellow player went blank. He looked at me and asked to stop the scene. As a side coach, I asked him what he thought Judas might say in this situation. He told me he didn't know who Judas was. Well, I'm sorry, but if you don't know who Judas was, there is little an improv teacher can do for you. I quizzed him on other current events, and he knew nothing. Keep studying, kids — it will only bring more depth to your work. Continue educating yourself and get as much life experience as you can. A high reference level is key to success on-stage.

Of course, intelligence isn't all it takes. Having confidence and being nonjudgmental are also traits that make a good improviser. This type of person will share the work with his friends, accept everything that is given him, and make it work. He hears from his heart as well as his ears. Confidence brings about calmness. With that comes the ability to think and take the time to come up with the best response possible, rather than a quick silly joke. The work is a tad slower because it is being processed in the brain, and the response comes from a place of emotion.

How to Be a Better Improviser

I like to tell my students to watch the shows and take a good hard look at the players who are more experienced than they are. Think to yourself, "What does that person do that I can't do?" Then find a way to learn to do that very skill either on-stage or in a class. One of our teachers, who happens to be one of the best improvisers around, is Miles Stroth from

The Family. He always admired the way his teammate Adam McKay used to narrate scenes. He felt that was a skill he did not have and took it upon himself to begin narrating on-stage. He began looking at all the other players and challenging himself to do the things that they could do. As soon as he mastered the skills of one player, he moved on to the next. He soon became an accomplished player.

We offer musical classes here at i.O. and one student in particular impressed me. The majority of the students who take this class are great singers who feel comfortable creating musical pieces on-stage. When I saw this one young man, I was surprised. I said, "Tom, I had no idea you were musically inclined." He said, "I'm not. I'm scared to death of it. So I figured I'd better learn how to do it if I want to be on-stage." That young man won my respect for facing his fear.

I always encourage my students to watch the more advanced players, as there is so much to learn from watching. Students seem to learn faster when they see what it is we are trying to achieve.

Mike Myers described what it's like watching a good player who is working organically.

When you're watching someone who is good, they never say no, they always say "yes" – "yes, and." And there isn't an ounce of sweat on them. It's not a grabby forced feeling. It's a looking upwards and receiving feeling. It's completely organic, and it's operating on the level of its latest offering. And there's channeling involved. When you see a great improv comedian, he's channeling, and that's exciting. It's almost like a trance. And it's not an intellectual process, although when you get stuck — and when you're out of trance — there are intellectual things to do to get back into the trance. It's speaking in tongues with full abandon, and you get high from that.

Rachel Dratch of *Saturday Night Live* says something remarkably similar to Mike's comments regarding the magic of this art form, "When it's working well, it's almost like channeling. You're saying lines before you realize that they're funny. The lines come out — people are laughing, and you're thinking, 'how did I think of that?' It's out of your control." Tim Meadows also agrees that improvisation can be magical, "It's like sitting in a room with a bunch of people, and you all say the same thing at the same time. You're in the same frame of mind, and you're all thinking the same way."

Have High Goals for Your Work

Del told us about a man named Dario Foe who won a Pulitzer Prize for a play he had written. In an interview, Mr. Foe revealed that his play was, in fact, improvised. That means, folks, we are capable of improvising something worthy of a *Pulitzer Prize*. Del used to tell us that while we may not always achieve this lofty goal, we should at least aim for it. He would always say, "Lead your target." He explained that when a hunter is about to shoot a bird, he would always aim a little further than where the bird was in his sight. By the time he shot, the bird would be where he was aiming. That is called "leading the target." So, if we aim a little higher, we may not always hit our target, but the work will be a little better.

CHAPTER 5:
Follow the Fear

I always tell my new students that they share the same character flaws, which is why they signed up for a class in improvisation. They pay money to hurl themselves into the state of the unknown. They pay to put themselves on the spot. They are risk takers. Those are the kind of people I like to hang out with.

Let's face it. Improvisation is an art form that is both sadistic and masochistic. It's sadistic because the audience wants to see you in danger. They are too scared to get up there without a script themselves, but they love to see you on the edge. Yet, they do want to see you succeed.

And it's masochistic because you're willing to put yourself into an uncomfortable situation — not knowing what will happen to you. You trust that you and your friends will come out okay. And the true improviser actually enjoys this!!

Del always said to follow the fear in your work. It is good to be uncomfortable; otherwise there is no danger, no excitement, no growth. If there is a topic that makes you uncomfortable, don't avoid it if it comes up in the scene. There is nothing that you cannot discuss. Deal with it from your point of view. If you are afraid of doing something on-stage for fear of looking stupid or being judged, that really means you have come up against one of your own self-imposed boundaries. Those are the boundaries you must break through in order to grow.

The wonderful thing about improvisation is that if you create a character on-stage, the audience won't believe it is you. So you have the freedom to be anyone you want.

If there is something happening in your group work and the team has no idea what is going on, follow it — don't drop it. I remember seeing someone begin a scene by pacing on-stage. He wasn't sure what to do, but he knew the audience saw him start to pace, so he couldn't stop. He kept pacing, and someone joined him from behind. Instantly, the rest of the group joined them — all pacing back and forth on-stage. They didn't know why they were pacing. But they knew they couldn't stop. They had to heighten it and pace even more. They had to heighten it to find out why they were pacing. It suddenly transformed into an angry circle of picketers. They followed through with their action. Too often students are afraid to follow their fear and heighten something for fear of looking stupid. Susan Messing, a favorite teacher to the masses here at i.O., says it best, "The worst thing that might happen if you look stupid is that people might laugh, and, since we are doing comedy, that's not a bad thing."

Many new students ask how to handle being nervous on-stage. Amy Poehler discussed this in a piece for our in-house newsletter. She was asked if she gets nervous when doing "The Weekend Update" on *Saturday Night Live*. She replied, "I think it's glorious to be nervous. Being nervous is great! How often do we get nervous on a daily basis? Being slightly nervous means you care, and you're alive, and you're taking some kind of risk. Hooray for being nervous! A friend told me to substitute the word 'excitement' for 'nervous.' That way you acknowledge the physical feelings without putting a negative spin on things. So to answer your question, sometimes I still get so *excited* about 'Update' that I want to throw up."

I remember when our very first team, the pioneers of long-form improvisation, Baron's Barracudas, learned a valuable lesson about being too comfortable on-stage. This was a hilarious team that was always fun to watch on-stage. One of the reasons they were so good had to do with one of their teammates, named Kim "Howard" Johnson, the same gentleman who edited my first book. It seemed that Howard, as we fondly called him, would always initiate games that would put the team into a tizzy. Whenever he came forward to initiate the game, a look of fear would appear on their faces as they stood behind him. They even began, as a joke, to pass out imaginary crash helmets and strap them on as soon as Howard would step forward. This delighted the audience because they knew the team was in trouble. Then Howard would initiate a game and say something like, "And now — the history of beds. First we have the trundle bed." In a sweeping gesture, he would motion to the team to become a trundle bed. In a state of frenzy, they would form a horizontal line, holding hands with their backs to the audience. They'd lie down on the floor and, in unison, do a backwards sommersault. The audience would cheer. They had become a trundle bed. Night after night, Baron's Barracudas would band together to overcome any obstacle that Howard might set up for them. One day, the group came to me. They couldn't take the pressure anymore. They wanted Howard off the team. I told them that I would never force a team to play with someone if they didn't want to, but I warned them that taking Howard off their team would be their downfall. They chose to ignore my warning, and as a group they asked Howard to step down from the team. Their very next performance was perhaps the dullest show they ever had. There were some funny scenes, but there was no danger — no risk taking. They were extremely comfortable and no longer fun to watch. They didn't even

Left to Right: Dave Pasquesi, Steve Burrows, Brian Crane, Bill Russell, John Judd, Honor Finnegan. Middle: Kim Howard Johnson and Judy Nielsen.

look like they were having fun. They realized the function Howard filled on that team. They apologized and asked him back. Howard forgave them, as the work was the most important thing. Baron's Barracudas were back, and once again they were following their fear.

The Sphere of the Frisbee

By the same token, Baron's Barracudas had a right to expect their teammate to initiate games that they could justify and play. Del used to teach us that when making initiations, make sure they weren't so far out that our fellow players couldn't catch them. He used to call this lesson "The sphere of the Frisbee." He would give the analogy of two people playing Frisbee. It's fun to see a player throw the Frisbee just out of someone's reach. The player has to stretch or perhaps jump to catch it. That certainly makes the game more interesting. But if the player were to throw it far off to the right instead of straight ahead — so far that it was impossible to catch — the game would come to a halt. In improvisation, make interesting moves, make your fellow player reach, but keep it within the sphere of the Frisbee.

CHAPTER 6:
The Kitchen Rules

IMPORTANT CHAPTER — READ TWICE!

Here's a little ditty for you history buffs. The rules that make improvisation so successful today were created by Del Close and some of our great improvisational pioneers in Elaine May's kitchen one night after a performance of The Compass Theater. According to Del, there were a lot of problems in the show that night. They went back to Elaine's apartment and asked one another, "Why the hell isn't this working?" Del said, "Well, for one thing, when you said we had a flat tire and I asked for the jack so that I could fix the tire, you gave me an argument. Maybe if you would have said 'yes *and* here's the spare,' we would have been on our way again." They all agreed they had to stop the arguing to get the scenes to forward. The **"Yes and" theory** was born.

It was then Del realized that there was a way to analyze the work and pose the right questions to figure out why something worked or didn't work. He began to develop the methods that we teach at i.O. today that tangibly steer our performers in the right direction.

Agreement

As I wrote in my first book, I don't teach rules because I am a fascist who wants you to do things my way. The rules as I teach them are basically the fundamentals to understanding how the art form is played successfully. Once you understand the techniques that make you successful on-stage, you no longer think of them as rules. You just understand how to be a good improviser. Let us substitute the word "rules" with the word "tools." One of the tools that makes improvisation successful on-stage is agreement. The agreement to the situation helps the players find their relationship in the scene. If you do not have that tool, you will have an argument, and the scene will not move forward. Nothing interesting will transpire on-stage. Agreement is a tool you must always use if you want to succeed. Not because it is a rule, but because that is how the game works. If you tell your fellow player that he is your father, then he is your father. It's no fun to be denied in your initiation. Our job is to honor one another's ideas. Remember, too, the audience comes to enjoy a show and escape their own lives for a couple of hours. They don't want to see you argue and be reminded of how miserable they sometimes are in their everyday existence.

While we are on the subject of agreement, I want to heighten a few ideas that were presented in *Truth in Comedy*. I discussed the importance of agreement and gave an excellent scenic exercise to teach agreement. The exercise is called "The Conflict Scene." In it, you are basically shown how to find agreement through a situation where there would normally be conflict. This exercise is perhaps one of the most important exercises in teaching agreement, as it shows that the scene is really about the relationship of the players and not about the conflict. The scene may begin with a man and a woman both wanting to pick up a check, but may become a scene about a male chauvinist who expects the woman to be the weaker sex. This is all discovered through the agreement to find the relationship in the scene. What we are really agreeing to is the situation in the scene. Very often, students who come here from other schools are confused about this point. They think the concept of agreement means you must agree to everything that is said in the scene. That's not true. We aren't asking you to sacrifice your integrity and say yes to everything that is said on-stage. We are agreeing to give what the other actor is asking for, and that could mean agreeing to say *no*. For example, there was a scene I once initiated on-stage where I was cowering in fear of my fellow player. While being very afraid of him physically, I verbally begged my "father" for some food. This was a strong initiation where one player was letting the other player know that she wanted him to be a mean, abusive father. He agreed to the initiation by saying, "No food for you today. Back in your cage." This was a correct response. This is what confuses beginning improvisers. How can this be right? I asked for food, and he said no. Isn't this conflict? No — it is agreement. The *character* said no, but the *actor* agreed to the situation of being a mean, abusive father. We must learn to read between the lines to hear what the actor is asking for and not be confused by the words that are being said. Del use to say, "Listen to the music as well as the words." This is why we take our scenes nice and slow. We have to take the time to read between the lines and think about what is being asked of us. Often we aren't saying what we appear to be saying. This is a real thinking-man's game, so slow down and play to the top of your intelligence. You must realize that the agreement is to what the *actor* asks for — not the *character*.

Throw Out the First Thought

There is another reason why we take our scenes slow. Del always told us to throw out our first thought when we are about to respond in a scene. The first thought is usually a knee-jerk reaction to what was just said to us. The second thought would be better, and the third would probably be the best and the most intelligent. So, allow one another time to think in your scenes. It will be worth waiting for. With practice, the ability to think this way will allow you to access the third thought as quickly as possible.

Support

There are teachers who believe that support is not important and that it is more important to take care of yourself than the other player. I do agree that it is important to take care of yourself on-stage. You certainly don't want to be a burden. But the problem that occurs when people are only taking care of themselves is that they are so wrapped up in their own idea that they aren't supporting the ideas of the rest of the group. When others play in this style with i.O. people, we invariably find we need to dance around them and justify all the weirdness they are creating because they have given themselves their own inner dialogue. Suddenly, we have to do all the work, and they become a burden.

At i.O., we believe that the only way to look good is to make one another look good by justifying one another and taking care of one another's ideas. That means that everything we hear is the most important idea in the world. We will be affected by it, use it, and heighten it. This is ensemble work, and either we all sink, or we all swim.

CHAPTER 7:
Separate but Equal –
Women in Improvisation

I am often asked to speak on the role women play in improvisation. Many new female performers feel like they are victims on-stage or that they are forced into the cliché roles of the housewife or girlfriend. I can understand why women feel that way. Long, long ago, when there was just Second City, the casts were traditionally two women and four men. The women were stereotyped as housewives or girlfriends. One was usually pretty while the other was usually funny looking and was played as the comic foil. It was as if talent wasn't an issue; they just had to fit the costume. They didn't seem to be a major part of the show. In fact, Del, who was the director there for twelve years before he met me, had a reputation for being a misogynist. This wasn't exactly true. He didn't hate women. What he hated was stereotypes. The woman who made lemonade and supported her husband's point of view in every scene just plain bored him. But he loved performing with Elaine May, and he flipped over Betty Thomas, whom he picked for the main stage himself. These women had a voice and were anything but stereotypical. They won his respect. Over the years, gender roles have been thrown out the window. Women have been coming to the forefront to prove that they are equally formidable players and to dispel the myth that improvisation is just a boy's club.

I do not consider myself a teacher of women or men. I teach players, and the advice is really the same for both genders. You are not a girl or a boy. You are an integral part of a whole. You must do what is best for the scene at that moment. You may be a prostitute in one scene and a C.E.O.

in the next. Everything handed to you is a gift. Saying no to this gift is denying the possibility of something magical happening. Still, no matter what character is handed to you, you can make strong choices on how you wish to play that character. You are in control. Keep your integrity high. Don't allow yourself to feel like a victim on-stage. I know it is easy to feel that way when much of the time women are outnumbered by male players on-stage. Do not get into the mindset that an initiation from a man is meant to be disrespectful. It has nothing to do with you. But, again, it is what you do with the initiation that makes the scene.

I recall a performance when a woman was on-stage. Two men entered, and the first man said, "Honey, I brought a friend home for dinner." The woman's reply was, "That's fine, dear, but I asked you to call me Madam President when we are not alone." There is always a way to control your own fate in your scene.

After reading this chapter in advance of publication, alumni Amy Poehler, of *Saturday Night Live*, commented that women who use their power on-stage are really interesting, "when they take it for themselves, they are eventually easily given it by other players."

One of the most touching scenes that stands out in my memory came from an initiation that would have made most new female players feel victimized. It was a lovely scene with Stephnie Weir of *MADtv* and her husband, Bob Dassie. Bob started the scene with Stephnie by saying he cashed his bonds from his Bar Mitzvah to buy himself a prostitute. He handed her the money. Stephnie replied, "You're thirteen? Me too."

She made a lovely choice to be this sweet little girl in a sad situation. The chemistry between these two characters made for a touching, poignant scene.

Stephnie has never been a victim on-stage. Neither have any of the other women from i.O. that we now see on stage and screen. They were always in charge and willing to use the stage to explore the ways that men and women integrate.

Women, you should not feel insecure. Feel good about yourselves. Women are actually better at this work than men.

They are more giving, caring, and nurturing on-stage. Amy believes they are usually better listeners, too. That may not always be true, but Amy recalls Rachel Dratch being the best listener she ever met. "She never forgets a name," Amy says of Rachel.

We had an amazing group called Jane a few years ago. It was an all-female team that was so wonderful to watch. Something happened in their performance that you didn't see on other teams. There was a calmness on-stage. They were content in working slowly, editing, transforming, and building things in a beautiful way. There was a feminine touch to the work. They liked playing without men, but their work wasn't about bashing men. They just felt that men improvised like they were playing football: fast and rough. The women of Jane wanted to take their time. It was a unique team, and since then many female groups have formed at i.O. to follow in their footsteps. It's a great opportunity for women to share ideas and feel like they aren't being steamrolled by men. That's fine, but just remember — anyone can be a steamroller. Amy Poehler recalls her time as director of Jane, "I was impressed by the trust and camaraderie of women playing together. There is something magical about that. But, also, a team with men and women working together and making everyone forget who they are and what they look like — that is awesome." She adds, "Women shouldn't be afraid to be physical, either. I remember playing a scene where I was a girl excited that her cool Uncle Jimmy came to visit. [Matt Walsh, from *Upright Citizen's Brigade*] I jumped all over him, and we rolled around on the stage. Use your size to your advantage. Make them forget you're small."

Amy Poehler and Tina Fey were on a team together here at i.O. called Inside Vladimir. I asked Amy about her experiences with the men she played with. She said, "Tina and I were lucky to be on a team of men who instantly played with us. We never felt restricted in what we could be. We [even] had a sleepover ... As the two women on the team, Tina and I always played well together because there was trust. Trust is so important in any group or scene. You have to trust that people will respect your boundaries, just like in life."

My last piece of advice for female performers, in addition to keeping your integrity high, is to look proper on-stage. If you look professional, you will play that way. Wear comfortable clothes that are not too tight-fitting and that are flattering to your size. Wear nice, soft-sole shoes that are easy to move around in and quiet when you walk on-stage. I have seen some horrifying outfits on-stage that have resulted in some embarrassing moments for women. I remember one woman who wore low-rider jeans on-stage. She sat sideways in a scene and exposed her rear end to half of the audience. It took a while to gain control of things after that moment. I'll let Amy make the last point on this issue as well, "Women should wear shirts that keep their boobs in. It's distracting if you're worried they are going to fall out."

Maintain Your Integrity

While I'm on the subject of keeping your integrity high, many questions have arisen regarding dealing with racial issues on-stage. We have a responsibility to say something in our work. Our job is not to just play a racist on-stage but to make a statement about racists through your character. Many people get confused about this and come off looking like racists and offend the audience. Del always told us that we wanted our laughs to come out of respect for our work — not contempt. The best example is Carroll O'Connor as Archie Bunker. As an actor, he made a statement about racists through his character. We were able to understand that he thought racists were ignorant through his behavior. That is our job. If you are an African-American, you are not supposed to be forced to play the low-status slave in a scene about slavery. Be higher status. Be smarter than the master. Make a statement through your work.

Before you finish this book, you will probably be hit with the term "play off the top of your intelligence" ten times. But it is so important to do that if you want to gain respect and succeed in this art form. Your character can be a racist, a slave, a drunk, a stoner, even mentally challenged — just make sure they are motivated characters with strong choices. As a performer, you must keep your integrity and dignity on-stage. If you lower yourself to play a low-status person for no reason but to insult, you insult both your scene partner and the audience.

CHAPTER 8:
Character through Environment and Movement

There is nothing more joyous than watching a character come to life in an environment that is being created on the spot by a performer. When the performer sees his environment in his own mind's eye, we the audience see it, too. Of all the performers I have known, Pete Hulne, of Beer Shark Mice, is the undisputed king of the physical world on-stage. For him, being physical is a necessity and not something to fear. I asked Pete to write the following essay for my book, as I thought it would be fun to get some helpful hints from the master himself. Ladies and gentleman, it's an honor to introduce you to one of my favorite performers — as well as one of my dearest friends — Pete Hulne.

Being Physical

By Peter Hulne of Corky's Callback,
The Family, and Beer Shark Mice

When I get on-stage, especially if it's the first time, I like to look it over. As queer as this sounds, I like to survey the space and look at everything that I can use. If there are flats, a door or window, if I can jump off the stage, climb on anything — you get the picture.

When I look at a space, I see a white room. Then, I like to add my own pieces specific to the location. Others can add their choices, too, and you have to respect their choices as much as your own. Respect in improv, at least to me, is one of the most important things on the stage. (Trust goes without saying.) Then you can add to someone else's creation, no matter how strange.

When I enter into a scene I like to, first, know where I am. So if I don't have a location, I set one up immediately.

"I can't believe Grandma's house has these naked men posters on the wall!"

Name the location; you've given your partner and you a much easier scene now that you both know where you are. Once I know the location it's easy. The reason being is that it will help me to add to a scene and also play a character with a point of view.

If you're in an airport, let's say, the things that you can do are boundless. There's always something to do. You don't have to be the funniest, most clever person in the world to make a scene work. Why?

Well, everyday occurrences are just as funny:

- •The taxi that gets you to the airport
- •The Sky Cap guys at the curbside check-in
- •The priest/religious person asking for money
- •The ticket takers
- •The security guards operating the metal detector
- •The coffee kiosks

That's just a few. Everyone has had their own experiences in an airport. Draw from them. Take and use what you know and heighten it.

I like to go for the not-so-recognizable thing, so I might have gone to one of those metal suitcase carriers, paid my money, and had a silent fight on-stage getting it to come out of the rack. Then, when I finally get it out, I have a bum wheel, and the scene continues with the craziness of the Mayor's suitcases constantly falling off. Who knows? Everyone has their own take on a scene. I say touch things, use things, ask about things. Set up your "where." If you don't know where you are, name where you are.

I come into a scene and I almost automatically set up boundaries. Not to confuse my partner, but to help them understand where they are and who I am.

If I'm in a kitchen, I first make everything downstage to the audience. The sink is in the middle of the stage, fridge and stove are on either side, and cabinets are everywhere else.

The reason I make everything down and off stage is because I don't want anyone walking through my creation. I get mad when people disrespect my space work. It also has to change the scene. If this person can walk through objects then he is supernatural. Plus, I don't want to be upstage with our backs or profile to the audience.

I think it's important to always listen to your scene partner and to take from them what they have set up. It's all building blocks; you put one down, and then I set one on top and so on and so on. If you know where you are ... you know what you can do to make a scene work.

I have often tried to analyze why Pete Hulne is so adept at physical creation. One of the reasons is that he was always fascinated by mimes. As to his penchant for initiating that physical level of playfulness with his teammates on-stage, he credits that to being a twin. As a twin, he has always had a playmate. He and his twin brother, Pat, would always create things together, so he was forming the group mind at an early age. When taking classes at i.O., he was particularly taken by our ideas of group work and commitment to the physical world.

Let us view a brief montage from The Beer Shark Mice piece to once again see the joyous physical world of Pete Hulne.

Watch the Beer Shark Mice Sequence on the DVD

I have seen wonderful moments where a strong environment has pulled the audience into a new reality. Alumnus Rich Talarico recalls one such moment when he performed here on his Harold team called Mr. Blonde: "We were doing a scene in which we were playing a family of Italian acrobats. While we all pretended to be up on a high wire, I heard the audience gasp as we almost fell. That moment was so powerful for me because a room full of people bought into our pretending."

The curriculum at i.o. has always been touted as the best for so many reasons. One of the reasons is our philosophy on the levels of commitment a player must have on-stage. A player must commit one hundred percent to his objects, just as he must be one hundred percent committed to the scene. At the same time, he is one hundred percent committed to playing the relationship that is being initiated while committing one hundred percent to the environment. Not to mention the one hundred percent commitment the players must make to one another as improvisers and teammates.

I have already mentioned Susan Messing. She is a performer here at i.O., and she is also one of our best teachers. Years ago, Susan created an excellent curriculum that supported the teachings of i.O. We created an entire level in the program to accommodate her curriculum. Susan is a great force behind many of our students, and I felt it equally important to hear from her as we take the ideas of the physical world on-stage further.

I must warn you in advance. The reason Susan is a great teacher is she says whatever is on her mind. She doesn't censor herself. She writes like she talks, she talks in run-on sentences, and she swears like a sailor. But she has a lot to say. Introducing Susan Messing ...

Be Happy. Move in Character.

By Susan Messing

I have always believed that scenes are about people in worlds, and a Harold is just a little world where lots of people can meet and have lots of fun together. However, more times than I can remember, I have watched people on-stage, standing in the middle of an abyss, making generalized statements like "*This* is fun." I am watching and thinking, "I sure don't know what *this* is, and it sure as hell *isn't* fun." But how do you generate information and create worlds when you see nothing? How do you turn off the tiresome inner monolog that's telling you that you suck, your scene's stupid, and you forgot to turn off the coffee maker when you left your apartment? I have heard that in "truthful" improvisation, as long as you can authentically portray yourself on-stage, everything is gold. Unfortunately, the master of the "authentic" me argues, judges myself and others, and fixes your problems. Many of these charming characteristics have helped to ruin comedy on any given day. Besides, I didn't necessarily start improvising to be *me*, anyway. I've got to do that twenty-three hours a day. There are the shows in which my goal is to be comfortable in my own skin, but I continue to embrace the opportunity to explore people and worlds that are different from my regular existence. It's time for some seven-year-old make-believe, but this time with adult sensibilities and, if I'm lucky, a piano player to score the happenings.

Fine, then. I'm going to try on something new. But what? And how? I remember a student who told me that she was going to do an improv show where she would lead with this wacky character that she had been developing in her spare time. She had a catchphrase that she thought was so funny that she cracked herself up describing it. Later, I asked her how her show went. She described it as a nightmare. "I initiated my wacky lady and had a premise for her. Unfortunately, my partner spoke first and said something that I couldn't figure out how to jive with my wacky lady. So I started arguing with him about his plot line, and I put out a paragraph or so of exposition which I didn't believe and couldn't remember and then he called me out on my wackiness and then I wanted to crawl into a hole and kill myself." Fun, huh? And, oh yeah, that's called "write a sketch, e-mail it to your friends, memorize it, add a few more jokes, and call it a day" comedy. It's not improvisation.

When I started improvising in the days when a mimed CD player was still new, I remember a guy who used to post his "character list" on the back of the flat that held up our stage. Seriously, this guy had about fifteen characters with titles like "old man with pipe" and "Iranian at Seven-Eleven." Even in my own personal newbie hell, I knew something was amiss. If the sky's the limit why would someone only have fifteen characters? I'm only limited by my *lack* of imagination and *fear* of appearing stupid. If the *only* thing that I can truly control in a scene is *me,* then there's got to be an easy and fun way for me to get inspired to try on a new human being. So I'm going to *do* something at the top of the scene that's going to excite and inspire me to enjoy the ride.

If I lead with my hips and that makes me feel like a supermodel, then no one will have the audacity to tell me that I'm *not* a six-foot-two supermodel (at least on-stage). Why? Because I can be anyone I want to be, and if you're watching and I'm enjoying the hell out of this world, chances are you will too. Joy is contagious. When you organically initiate a scene by heightening a body part, it might even naturally change your voice. Now your perspective's different, and you're giving yourself permission to share this person's views, and oh my God, I'm talking like a supermodel, and everyone's treating me like a supermodel, and sweet baby Jesus, I'm enjoying being this person so much, and I love everything that's coming out of my partner's mouth who, by the way, called me his lawyer, and that's cool cause now I'm a supermodel-like lawyer, and our room is so fun to play in, and lookie here what I found in this cabinet that's there to support our relationship, and it's effortless, and I can't wait to be this person again, and lookie, lookie time has passed, and it's so easy, and I'm so happy, and wheeee!

The "game" in terms of your character is your characteristics. People have personal tics or a particular way they stand. Repeat that sucker, and it's starting to feel like that's something you always do. Do it more, and you'll discover *why* you hold yourself the way you do. Normally, I tuck my melons in. When I push them out I feel like a whole new lady. My partner can initiate a plot or name this person anything, and I still get to be this person because that's what I get to own. No one can manipulate my spine but *me*. I discover the rest of the scene together with my partner. Even changing up my eyes changes me. If I hold my mouth differently than I normally do, I speak differently than I did, and it even changes up my emotion. It's hard for me to disagree when I start a scene with a smile on my face.

Truth in comedy in character has responsibilities. At i.O., if my energy level is too "out there," I will have the tendency to look crazy or mentally disabled. Nothing wrong with that, but I'm playing in a grounded reality here, so I adjust my inner dial to feel different but not like a cartoon. That way, I can play *with* people instead of having the entire scene be about my wacky lady. By the way, I'm also turning down my internal monolog that tells me how much I suck as an improviser. People don't pay good money to watch us judge ourselves. If my face indicates "I suck," I can guarantee that the audience will think, "Then why are you on-stage?" Hate yourself later. Enjoy the ride *now*.

I had a great acting teacher in college, David Downs, who made our class go to the zoo and pick an animal and "do" their spines in class. This meant to take on the characteristics of the animal. Then we had to make the animal evolve into a person. I guess I could try that if I got the urge. Or perhaps I can imagine I'm wearing a certain piece of clothing. Most people would stand differently in a tube top than in a formal gown. If you stand like you're in a tube top but you're really in a formal gown, that might be fun too. No matter what, the more ways I can access shedding my skin to try on another human being, the happier I am because I'm creating my fate through a purely organic gesture that will inspire me. It'll inspire my scene partner, too.

What if I don't take care of myself at the top of the scene by doing something with myself and my world? My mentor, Mick Napier, gave me a lovely quick fix by suggesting that I match the energy of my partner. That gesture immediately makes me feel like we're in the same world already. Even matching facial expressions feels like we're connecting. I would much rather *move* and discover something about myself or be inspired by my partner's body position as an organic way to begin than have to stand around and invent "clever," which, more often than not, isn't.

"Do something" means *move*. Move unlike yourself, and you might find someone new in you. It *is* that time to take that silly dance or movement or yoga class. Pay some person to touch you and get out the physical kinks that might be limiting your mobility. When your body's loose, it unleashes your imagination. Walk the catwalk. You look stunning.

Group Mind through Movement and Your Responsibility to Support the Lemming Cause

I once saw a Harold where the team got the suggestion, "dance," so they all started dancing really badly. All of their faces telegraphed, "Isn't it funny to dance badly?" The audience responded like crickets chirping in an empty Hollywood Bowl. I learned a valuable lesson in that moment. When you indicate that something is funny, it really isn't. At i.O., we talk about playing to the "top of our intelligence," and if we translate that into movement, we move to the *best* of our ability. Creating beautiful scenic pictures together is beautiful to watch. And let me add, if you are uncomfortable about moving in a way that's new to you, once again, the worst thing that's going to happen if you move to the best of your ability and you still appear stupid, is you'll be making some sweet comedy.

I hear people dissect "group mind," as if it's some profound abstract theory that we all hope to trip over and unearth, but to achieve teamwork, it's as simple as me agreeing to the group's energy by *joining* it. That's how I can enjoy being an integral part of a whole. Energy is contagious, good and bad. Throwing yourself into the group mix alleviates so much of the feeling of being alone. Sometimes it's a huge *relief* to be a "lemming." When I add myself into the group dynamic, I know that we can build something together that I would never be able to achieve on my own. "Art by committee" is incredibly satisfying. It entails me to mirror my friends and *add* to the beautiful picture that has been created so far.

Have you ever watched a group scene where someone feels left out and then says, "*Stop*"? Through my years of watching and participating in thousands of scenes, I have learned that what that improviser is *really* saying is, "Stop the scene. I want to get off!" or, "Stop the scene until I can figure it out," or, "Stop the scene. Look at me! Look at me! No one's looking at me! I have no function. Validate me! Oh dear, everyone's looking at me. Now what?" This person has what I have lovingly named, "Frustrated Improviser's Disease," or FIDS. There's a lot of ways a person can get and share FIDS. There are entire books and online forums that address just that issue, but from a personal standpoint, in group work, I have found that FIDS used to come from the part of me that was a frustrated leader. *"C'mon, you guys!"* That's no fun to play with, ever. However, the fix for me was to relax and *join in* the predominant energy of the group. Immediately I felt as if I were on the same page as my friends, sharing *our* world, creating something gorgeous *together*, and then I was back on the fun ride. Other people need to pull up their energy in order to join the mix. I always notice the person holding up the back wall, terrified to join in with the other kids, and all I can say to you is, pull up your energy, sweetheart. You're not dead yet. Even if you're usually the most mellow person on the planet, what we need from you right *now* is to be responsible enough for yourself to check out your energy and adjust it to the group's immediate needs. After all, I can't manipulate your spine or energy level. That's *your* job. There's all the time in the world for you to be different and unique from the rest of the gang. Right now, all of us lemmings need to fall off the cliff together. If you *choose* to stand back and watch us plummet, you will notice that we just started flying to heaven, you lazy bum, and you just missed the ride of your life. Ever watch "the wave" being done at a football game? A simplistic gesture at best — get out of your seat, wave your arms up when it comes to you, sit down, and pick up your beer when you're done. You know who the $#@*%* is? It's the one who *stops* the wave.

Improv is a visual art. If you all want to stand around and just talk about it, wake me when you're done, as I can hear that stuff on the radio. Watching people *do* things and *discover* things is far more interesting than your verbal rantings. Even when the President makes a speech in The Rose Garden, nobody cares. They're far more interested in watching the fly buzz around his nose. So, what if you don't know how to contribute to a group dynamic? Match energy. More specifically, you can *add* to the world that's been created — or even initiate the world — instead of thinking, "What the hell do I do now?" Perhaps you need a semantic adjustment to rephrase your thought to, "Hmmm, what can I do to make this world prettier? This forest needs a tree. I will be that tree. Or, I will add a birdy to that tree. Now there's a birdy in a tree, and it's there because I did it." At least you moved your behind and contributed, and that feels good. The more you wait to add to the group, the more the jump rope turns into a large steel cable. If you keep waiting to jump in, you're probably still waiting. I hate watching people "wait" to have fun. Even more, I hate being that person.

Some years back I created a game called Busby Berkley. Basically, it's an organic dance built upon a simple yet committed physical initiation where people add, mirror, and balance stage pictures with symmetry and through commitment. Images appear and reappear, themes emerge, and every single improviser who has tried it on fully has looked *gorgeous* doing it. The uber-commitment alone creates lovely comedy. The *only* time it hasn't worked is when the participants don't commit. I had a class where they did a Busby Berkley and there was one guy who just wasn't buying it. Oh, he was on-stage with a partner, but his face completely had the "this is so stupid" smirk. When they were done, I didn't even have to yell at him, as his peers did it

69

for me. They were *furious* at him. He sheepishly said he "didn't understand the exercise," but he was outed for being the one who single-handedly *ruined* beauty. Truly, he did. By judging himself and everyone else, he got to be "different" and "unique." He also had the opportunity to have people dismiss him as a performer. But Susan, maybe he didn't really understand the exercise. Maybe he can't dance. Look, my daughter is a toddler, and she understands the exercise and doesn't have *judgment* that it's *stupid*, so she is a joy to watch.

Who's the $@%&$%? The one who *stops* the wave.

CHAPTER 9:
My Pet Peeves

This is actually a plea to emcees of improv shows or the first performer on-stage to speak to the audience. *Please don't beg the audience to clap and scream.*

Too often I see performers or emcees bound onto the stage, and, in an effort to "bring energy" to the stage, they say something like, "Let's hear it," in an effort to beg the audience to cheer and scream. Why? They haven't done anything deserving yet. This is not bringing energy to the players. I do not deny that the players will feed off the energy of the audience when they do something on-stage that induces the audience to cheer and scream. There is a sense of pride and appreciation that comes from knowing the audience is pleased with what you have done. Del used to say that such approval from the audience can be compared to mainlining speed. It's a rush. But forcing the audience to cheer is all smoke and no fire. You don't feel appreciated — you feel like a beggar. The excitement from the audience will come from within the show. Make your entrance with dignity. You don't have to scream and jump onto the stage.

A good example is The T.J. and Dave Show. When they start their show, they calmly walk on-stage and nod to the audience in a very distinguished manner. Their opening music gets the audience clapping on their own. T.J. then welcomes the audience and thanks them for coming, then merely says, "Trust us — this is all made up." There is no screaming, no huffing and puffing, no jumping up and down. But, believe me, there is a ton of energy on-stage.

You Always Do This! You Always Say That!

The other night I was watching The T.J. and Dave Show here at i.O. At the beginning of the very first scene, T. J. looked at Dave wide-eyed and said excitedly, "I can't believe this is really going to happen!" Dave matched his enthusiasm and said, "Can you imagine? Soon we will be rubbing shoulders with some of the most brilliant Nobel Peace Prize Winners in the world." The scene took off from there in a hilarious ball of energy. But can you imagine what would have happened if after T.J.'s first line Dave said, "Oh, this happens all the time"? The energy would get sucked out of the scene and ruin the excitement of the first time that something is happening. The initiation would be watered down. This is one of the most common mistakes made by new improvisers.

Let us see the characters in your scene handle a situation for the first time. If someone says, "I'm leaving you," we want to see how you are going to handle that traumatic situation right now. We don't want you to dismiss the importance of that initiation by saying, "You always say that when you are mad at me." Of course, the scene can still work if that happens because we are justifiers, and we must make everything work. The scene would then be about someone who is always breaking up. But another one of our responsibilities is to honor the other person's initiation and make it the most important idea we have ever heard.

This Is My First Day

Along with the previously mentioned line, "You always say that," there is another line I have heard approximately 12,394 times during my twenty-five years of teaching: "*This is my first day.*" When I hear a player say this line, I know right away he is verbally announcing that he is about to play an incompetent character on-stage. He does this because he finds himself pretending to have an occupation that he knows nothing about. If he finds himself a surgeon in an operating room, he is about to panic because he knows nothing about surgery. Don't ask us to believe something that you wouldn't buy yourself. How realistic is it to believe that a surgeon who is about to operate on someone really doesn't know how to do it? The good news is you don't need to know anything about surgery. We don't want you to talk about what you're doing anyway, so you don't have to give us a play-by-play description of your surgical procedures, nor do you have to pretend that you don't know how to do your job. The scene is not about what you are doing. It is more a discovery about your character and how he relates to others in the operating room. Play that character to the best of your ability.

Don't Play Cliché

Mike Myers remembers Del believing there should be no difference between the street and the stage. Mike recalls, "Del didn't like TV or parody type things. He preferred fresher observations that weren't filtered through the culture. He felt that 'in general' was the enemy of art and that *God* was in the details."

And, in that same vein, Del believed there was no difference between the street and the stage where intelligence was concerned. Del always said that it took a lot of intelligence to survive in the city. Use the same intelligence that you use on the streets to survive. Bring that same intelligence to the stage.

No Talking On-Stage

When you are on-stage performing a long-form piece of any kind, it is so very important to pay attention to every word on-stage. Even if you are off to the side and not in a scene, what is being said will affect you later on. You may find yourself in a situation where you don't remember a character's name and you want to lean over and ask your fellow player. Or you may want to ask what he wanted you to do in a previous scene. Resist the temptation to talk. I sometimes see this on-stage when the players are off to the side and, on the most basic level, it is a problem because it steals focus. But more importantly, you are going to miss what is being said at that moment, and there is nothing worse than wondering what just happened on-stage while you were talking.

I remember a Harold that was going beautifully for the first half of the show. The first scene was an old married couple reading the newspaper at the breakfast table. It was an adorable scene where their relationship was based on the different stories they told each other from the newspaper. Scene two was about two young men who decided they wanted to be the best they could be. They were joining the Army and beginning basic training. In the second beat of the Army scene, the boys were about to experience their first parachute jump. They were scared. They did a great job as new performers by actually moving the scene forward by jumping out of the plane and opening their chutes. They did a lovely job of pretending to be blown about the stage as they slowly began their descent.

That scene was edited by the old couple who began once again to read the paper. The two army boys were off to the side of the stage. They began whispering to each other — possibly planning what might happen next. While they were talking to each other, the old man said to the woman, "Oh, look at this. Two young men were skydiving for their first time and were blown into some electrical wires and were electrocuted. How sad to be cut down in the prime of their lives." This was a wonderful initiation, as it went along with the theme the group was creating of making the best out of life.

The boys now would have had a choice to make. They could choose to not bring back their scene again because they were dead. Or we could have seen them happily blowing in the wind, pretending not to know what is about to befall them, perhaps even innocently pointing out the electrical plant in the distance. The problem was that the boys didn't hear the couple kill them off in their previous scene because they were talking offstage. They landed successfully, and unfortunately the audience was aware of the mistake that they didn't even know about until I gave them notes afterwards. For them, not talking on-stage was an important lesson learned.

Going Blue for a Laugh

One of the things that I have been proudest of is the reputation i.O. has for high-brow comedy. But once in a while, I see a newer performer "begging" the audience to laugh by trying to gross them out or using blue language that isn't necessary for the scene. Yes, you can get a laugh (or a groan) by picking your nose on-stage, or being crass, but, in my opinion, that's too easy. It comes off as a desperate attempt to shock the audience into some kind of a reaction. Don't lower your goals. As a performer, you are going to have to have more going for you than the ability to be raunchy. The people who have gotten the furthest in their performing careers are the ones who have managed to get their laughs in more creative ways.

CHAPTER 10:
From Improv to Writing

At i.O. we have been creating actors, improv coaches, directors, and as of the last few years, we are apparently creating writers as well. It's very rewarding to see how many of our performers are now being hired as writers for television shows like *The Daily Show, Saturday Night Live, Late Night With Conan O'Brien, MADtv*, and *The Colbert Report*, as well as movies on the big screen. But it isn't surprising. Our work is excellent preparation for the job.

Adam McKay, writer and director of *Anchorman*, says that improvisation is acting and writing at the same time; "Improvisers are writers who are writing on-stage." In that same vein, Mike Myers, who wrote the *Wayne's World* and *Austin Powers* films, claims that when writing, improv is indispensable; "Writing is improv at the typewriter." And it seems that he still has to follow the improv rules when writing; "You have to agree that when you have written something and they come to say you can't go to Thailand with your character — you say 'OK,' and you go to Palm Springs. If it can't be Palm Springs — it's the exterior of Malibu. You then agree and add to all the circumstances and limitations. Improvisation teaches you adaptability." Mike cited Del's analogy of the master Sufi weavers who would teach their apprentices to weave their baskets. When the apprentice would make a mistake, the master would weave the mistake into the pattern and make a more sophisticated pattern. Hence, there is no mistake. Adaptability!

Kevin Dorff, who writes for *Late Night with Conan O'Brien*, agrees with Mike that following the rules of improvisation helps in writing, "I think of ideas and things to write in the same manner that I construct improv scenes with people. I start off with something and start agreeing to my own idea and then forward and add to it. I really enjoy and I'm lucky to create with people who have this background. In fact, we're all from i.O., and that's half the staff. We speak the same language much the same way we do on-stage.

Andy Dick feels that improvisation is the most collaborative art form out there; "The scene in an improvisation will never be about what I want it to be about or what my partner wants it to be about. It's about what we both make it together. I love that." Andy loves to write in much the same manner. He will work with other writers who will play off his ideas. "I'm a little left of center though," says Andy, "so I handpick writers that are a little bit left of center like me."

Adam McKay has found that improvisation has also helped him as a director, "The great thing about directing is I get to use everything — my experiences as an actor, an improviser, and a writer all came together. There is enough un-chartered terrain in directing that you can make it up as you go along. I can totally create my own style of directing which I'd obviously like to be very improvisational and encourage the actors to mess around and try stuff. I really like that."

Tina Fey, head writer for *Saturday Night Live* and the writer of the film, *Mean Girls*, says, "The idea of honoring a suggestion when improvising is the way I approach writing. I can't think of this crazy stuff I get out of the air. I have to be responding to something in the news, or socially, or a character that someone has. I feel like I have to be honoring a suggestion in some way — the way I would be at i.O. Otherwise it feels self-indulgent to me. That's how i.O. influences my way of working."

Many performers try to write up scenes that were funny on-stage so that they can be used in a written show later on. That's a good process, but it is often difficult. Keep in mind that improvisation is enjoyable to watch because of the risk-taking involved. The audience has a great reaction because they know you took a chance in doing something on the spot, be it a rap or a dance. But in a written show, where the audience knows you have had a chance to write and rehearse, that same moment might not be met with the same reaction. Now that you've had time to prepare, that rap had better be perfect, and that dance had better be magnificent. There is less forgiveness from the crowd once you've had the opportunity to write.

The best way to tell if your writing is good is to get it up in front of an audience. That is the true test.

CHAPTER 11:
Advice to Future Performers

It is very exciting to me to see the increasing number of performers from i.O. and i.O. West who go on to become successful in the entertainment industry. Many people come to i.O. because they read that their heroes in comedy have started here, and they, too, want to be stars. It's very important that you know that the i.O. alumni who are stars did not come here because they wanted to be stars. They came here because of their love of the work. While they were here, they were absolutely devoted to performing as often as they could and taking classes as often as they could. As a result, they became the cream of the crop. I remember when Mike Myers was on the main stage at Second City but still never missed a Monday night class with Del at i.O. As a performer, he was always interested in learning more. The people who loved the work were the ones who were noticed. Del used to say that the people who come here with tunnel vision to be stars usually end up in community theater somewhere. Just be devoted to the work, take the time to get good, and the rest will take care of itself.

Some of our alumni have gotten themselves into trouble. We lost Chris Farley to drug abuse. I want to set the record straight, especially because there are a lot of drug references here in the book. We advocate staying clean and healthy. There are drug references in this book because we quote Del quite a bit, and, unfortunately, that was a big part of Del's life. We do not, however, encourage you to emulate his lifestyle. When John Belushi and Chris Farley died, Del believed they misunderstood some of his advice. Del used to say, "Burn brightly until you burn out," but he didn't mean to burn out in life. By the way, Del stopped doing drugs in memoriam of John Belushi.

I have watched Chris Farley and Andy Dick as well as other talented performers when they were at i.O. They would come off the stage after a great show, and they would be so excited that their feet weren't touching the ground. They were in a state of a natural high. They found excitement in the work. They would drink to calm their nerves before a show and then drink to celebrate after the show — sometimes to excess.

Later on, with success, they may have forgotten where that excitement came from, and they were trying to get it back. Where it once came from a live audience, it was now coming from alcohol and drugs.

When you are a working actor, remember that creating projects and performing live are ways to keep recreating that excitement for yourself. All of you must remember that you will never have done it all. Do not stop creating. The excitement is in the work.

And while I'm on the subject — create things that you are proud of. I remember having a conversation with Mike Myers during a time when he was having some legal problems regarding a movie he was making based on his Deeter character from *Saturday Night Live*. He cancelled the project because he wasn't happy with the way the script was turning out. The studio was less than pleased. Mike felt an obligation to his public; either the movie is good or it doesn't get made. I complimented him on his behavior despite the fact that he might get sued because of it. He said, "It is what I must do in order for my soul not to turn black."

Mike's advice to people who love the work was told in an interview during i.O.'s twentieth anniversary.

I never gave up or listened to people who told me I had no right to do this. You're in for a lot of rejection, and, in the early part of it, absolutely no money whatsoever. I'm very lucky. I also work very hard. I take this stuff very seriously. I know a lot of extremely talented people who didn't get as many breaks. The thing that keeps you going is not growing cynical. I can still call it an art form. I still believe in it. I still think it's good. If you don't achieve any success — or if you do achieve success — the work should be reward in itself. Getting to do this for a living is a major miracle.

Neil Flynn of *Scrubs* believes that luck is "preparation meeting opportunity."

When asked to pass down advice, Stephnie Weir of *MADtv* focused on the things that made her and her colleagues so successful in the work.

You really have to be willing to embrace what everybody is bringing to the table. That's when magic happens — when you accept what people are doing. Embrace their ideas and open yourself up to the many options that can happen on-stage. When you shut down and think, "That's not what I thought was going to happen on-stage," you bring it to a screeching halt.

The thing I realize about everybody I've worked with is they brought something that is their very own to the stage. They're not trying to model themselves after someone else or doing what they think will get them farther. But being true to yourself and bringing to the stage your life experience and what you have to offer up, that's the most valuable tool that you have. That is one of the keys to success.

i.O. Photo Album

Left to right: Pat Finn, Charna Halpern, and Neil Flynn during Chicago Improv Festival 8.

Left to Right: Jet Eveleth, Bob Kulhan, and Holly Laurent.

Amy Poehler at the i.O.'s 25th Anniversary. Photo by John H. Abbott, © 2005.

Left to right: George Wendt, Andy Dick, and Mo Collins at i.O.'s twenty-fifth anniversary. Photo by John H. Abbott © 2005

Rachel Dratch (left) and Charna Halpern at i.O.'s 25th Anniversary. Photo by John H. Abbott, © 2005.

Left to right: Rachel Dratch, Tina Fey, Charna Halpern, and Amy Poehler.

Charna Halpern and Mike Myers. Photo by John H. Abbott, © 2005.

Charna Halpern and Mike Myers on-stage. Photo by John H. Abbott, © 2005.

Andy Dick and Charna Halpern relaxing at i.O. West.

Andy Richter (left) and Fred Willard.

Andy Dick (left) and Tim Meadows in a scene from the i.O.'s twentieth anniversary.

Andy Richter performing at the L.A. Improv Festival at i.O. West.

The Armando Diaz Theatrical Experience in a scene at i.O. Photo by John H. Abbott, © 2005.

Left to right: Tammy Sagher, Sara Gee, Fred Willard, Craig Cackowski, Laura Kraft, and Andy Richter.

Blue Velveeta: Top row, left to right: Brian Blondell, Jay Leggett, Susan Messing, Mitch Rouse, Tom Booker, Brendan Sullivan. Bottom: Kevin Dorff.

Bob Dassie and Stephnie Weir of Weirdass.

Charna Halpern and Andy Dick at the i.O.'s twentieth anniversary.

Charna Halpern and Tim Meadows at i.O.'s twenty-fifth anniversary. Photo by John H. Abbott, © 2005.

Amy Poehler (left) and Charna Halpern.

Cast photo 2005. Photo by John H. Abbott, © 2005.

Dave Pasquesi (left) and T. J. Jagadowski.

Dave Koechner and Charna Halpern. Photo by John H. Abbott, © 2005.

The Family. Left to right: Ali Farahnakian, Adam McKay, Miles Stroth, Matt Besser, Ian Roberts, and Neil Flynn.

Del Close.

Del Close with cigar.

The many faces of Del Close.

Fish Stchick. Top row, left to right: Brian McCann, Pat Finn, Randy Hassan, Leo Ford, and Ian Gomez. Bottom row: Cici Lubin, James Grace, and Chris Farley.

Grime and Punishment. Left to right: Mick Napier, Madeline Long, Richard Label, Tim Meadows, and Dave Razowsky.

Left to right: Jack Halpern, Iris Halpern, Charna Halpern, Tim Meadows, and Andy Dick at i.O.'s twentieth anniversary.

Left to right: Fred Willard, Tami Sagher, Laura Kraft, Craig Cackowski, and Sara Gree.

Tequila Mockingbird. Bottom: Rachel Dratch. Second row, left to right: Dave Koechner, Noah Gregoropoulos. Third row: Leo Ford, Jimmy Carrane. Fourth row: Kevin Dorff. Fifth row: Brian Stack, Pat Finn.

The Reckoning. Front row, left to right: Brad Morris, Pat O'Brien. Second row: Charlie McCracken, Brian Jack, Jake Schneider, Jet Eveleth. Third row: Holly Laurent. Top row: Eddie Pina, Shad Kunkle, T. J. Jagadowski, Eric Hunnicut, and Beau Gowitzer.

Left to right: Mike Myers, Rachael Mason, Jimmy Carrane, Andy Dick and Mo Collins.

No Shame featuring Pete Gardner (top left), Dave Koechner (top right), James Grace (center), and Ellen Stone King (bottom center).

PLAY. Left to right: Holly Laurent, Damien Arnold, Jet Eveleth, Peter Grosz, Dan Bakkedahl, T.J. Jagadowski, and Deb Downing.

Part 3
History

CHAPTER 12:
The History of Charna and Del and Long-Form Improvisation

Jeff Griggs, a young man who performs and teaches at i.O., has recently come out with a new book written about his experiences with Del called *Guru*. When Jeff was a student here at i.O., he applied for what we call an internship, which basically means a student will work off his classes if he cannot afford to pay for them. For nineteen years, I had been the one to take care of Del. As my theaters in Chicago and L.A. grew, it became impossible for me to take care of every one of Del's needs. I thought it would be a great idea to give Del his own intern. Someone who would pick up Del once a week and drive him to the grocery store, to the bank — any errands Del had in mind for the week. I liked Jeff a great deal and thought he would be thick-skinned enough to handle Del. Del has been known to eat people alive, but Jeff seemed pretty brave. I asked Jeff if he would be interested in hanging with Del once a week and if he would be able to drive him around. Jeff jumped at the chance. His book, *Guru*, is based on these days with Del. It's a very fun book. I wrote the epilogue to the book, and I highly endorse it. By the way, it wasn't until I read the book that I learned Jeff didn't even have a car.

Many of the readers who have enjoyed Jeff's book have said that they would love to hear some of the stories I have with Del. A great deal has happened between me and Del in nineteen years, and maybe I can get Jeff to force me to sit down long enough to spill my guts. In the meantime, I thought I would jot down a few of the things that have happened between us as an addendum to this book to give you a little more insight into Del.

Del and Charna Get Together and Change the Face of Improvisational Comedy

In 1980, I had heard that David Shepherd, the founder of The Compass Theater, was in town. He was auditioning young actors for a play he was producing called *The Jonah Complex*. I had just read about him in Jeff Sweet's book, *Something Wonderful Right Away*. I knew of his importance in the history of improvisation, and I remembered reading that he had tried to start a comedy competition in Canada called ImprovOlympic. The competition involved different teams of improvisers competing in improvisational games that he had created for the competition. David mentioned in the interview that this competition really never got off the ground. The idea was very close to that of Comedy Sportz or Theatre Sports — both of which we really had not heard of yet in Chicago. I had just finished Players Workshop of Second City and formed a troupe called Standard Deviation. There were many other troupes around just like mine that had nowhere to perform due to the fact that we were not one of the six people working for Second City. There really was no improv community at the time, just a bunch of us wannabes who had nowhere to play. While driving home to the suburbs, I had the first epiphany I have ever had in my life. I knew I could successfully produce ImprovOlympic here in Chicago. There were countless people like me and the very talented Dan Castellaneta (now known for being the voice of Homer Simpson), who would kill to have a place to play. I got on the cloverleaf and immediately headed back to the city to try to meet Shepherd. The auditions were at Victory Gardens. I approached him about my idea, but David was only interested in having me audition for his play. I thought, "What the hell — I'm already here." I auditioned and got the role of God. Not too shabby. *The Jonah Complex* was a cool project. It was the story of Jonah and the Whale brought to modern times. The concept was that God calls on someone to give his message to the world and, of course, the person refuses to pass on that message for fear of being thought of as a crazy person. To David's credit, this was before the movie *Oh God!* with George Burns.

David always was ahead of his time.

During rehearsals, I convinced David to let me start ImprovOlympic here with him. The first year was very successful. We had teams of actors as well as identity teams, like the rabbis called "The God Squad" and the psychologists called "Freudian Slippers." We even had a media team with famous on air personalities called "Media Rare." It was David's idea that all these diverse people play together to celebrate one another's backgrounds.

While ImprovOlympic was having a great deal of commercial success, I was experiencing some personal problems with it. In addition to the fact that the non-professional teams had scheduling problems — like the rabbis who couldn't play on Fridays — I was quickly becoming bored with the games. It seemed like nothing new was happening. The same old jokes were being relied upon. I felt there had to be something more for improvisation besides games.

I had heard of a man named Del Close who was the Director at Second City for twelve years. There were rumors that he did not like me nor did he respect this thing called ImprovOlympic. Never mind the fact that he didn't know me and had never ever seen a show of mine. According to some of my friends who were students of his, his mind was made up.

One Halloween night, I heard there was going to be some kind of performance by Del Close and some of his students at an art gallery. I decided to check out this evil man who hated me — just to see what he was up to.

At the performance, he gathered his students in a circle and began to do something called "The Invocation." And, since it was Halloween, they decided to invoke demons. At the time, I was taking a class in meditation and had been taught to do something called "white lighting" yourself. It was a method of protecting yourself by imagining your body surrounded in white light. I thought that Del Close had a lot of nerve invoking demons without protecting the crowd that was standing around observing. After the very creepy performance, I decided to go up to him and give him a piece of my mind. He hated me anyway, so I had nothing to lose. To be honest, I didn't think he would know who I was. I said to him, "You had a lot of nerve invoking demons without protecting the audience." He responded in a condescending manner, "I protected the building." "You can't do that," I responded. He stared me down and said, "Yes, I can." I walked away in a huff. Now I hated him too.

A few months later I was even more bored with ImprovOlympic than before. I hated emceeing my shows as well as teaching the little games in class. If I saw one more gibberish translation, I was going to puke. It was then that I saw Del Close sitting in the lobby of CrossCurrents having coffee. CrossCurrents was where my shows were at the time. He was waiting for a meeting with the owner of the club. I decided that I was desperate. I thought if I could get him to teach a class maybe he could take us further in the art form. I had heard he was a genius at directing, so I had to make an attempt. I decided to overcome my fear of approaching him. Sure, we had a bad first meeting, but Del was famous for not remembering anyone and for always being high, so I doubted he would remember me from a few months ago. I went up to his table and asked if he would like to make two hundred dollars and some pot. He looked up at me and asked, "What do I have to do?" I said that I wanted him to teach one three-hour class. He took a long drag from his cigarette, which kept me in suspense, waiting for an answer.

"Can I do anything I want?"

"Yes," I said. I was now confident he didn't remember me, as he seemed pretty friendly.

Then, he looked at me with the same stare he gave me that night a few months ago. *"Can I invoke demons?"*

I froze. He remembered me. But it was too late to show my fear. I said he could invoke demons.

He then said he would teach that night at 7:00 p.m.

Del taught the invocation that evening and explained what it was he was really doing on Halloween night. The exercise was wonderful (See *Truth in Comedy*). Del, on the whole, was inspiring and exciting. The class was an eye-opening experience for me and my fellow players. We realized, basically, that we knew nothing. We had so much to learn.

After the class, I took Del out for coffee. I told him of my real reasons for asking him to do the class. I hated the games and wanted to see what was next for improvisation. He looked at me in surprise and said, "Well, you're not a twit after all." I thanked him for that "lovely" compliment. We began to discuss his goals for improvisation and his frustrations with Bernie Sahlins, who owned Second City at the time. Bernie wouldn't let Del experiment with the work because Bernie was already making millions on the Second City shows and didn't feel the need to experiment. Del thanked Bernie for giving him a place to recover from the '60s and gave his notice.

Del decided he liked me and made me an offer. He told me there was something he had been working on since the '60s. It was called "Harold." "At this point," he said, "it is basically un-teachable and unplayable, as there is no structure. But if you close down ImprovOlympic and we begin working on this thing, you and I just may change the face of improvisational comedy." I could not contain myself. I shook hands on it without thinking.

At our first rehearsal, we experimented with some of my players. We decided that if we took some of the games from the old ImprovOlympic and inserted them into the Harold as a structure, we might be able to figure this thing out. One of the games I did love from the old ImprovOlympic was The Time Dash, a three-part scene where the beginning, middle, and end were separated by light cues. We decided that three time dashes would be the main structure for the Harold. Other short games could be included at the whim of the performers. Del said that we were not eliminating short-form, we were just creating a meta-game that ate short-form games. Long-form improvisation was born.

Del has often thanked me for putting his life's work on-stage. Del and I did, in fact, change the face of improvisational comedy. In addition to that, we changed each other's lives.

CHAPTER 13:
Tennessee Williams Meets Del

When I met Del, he was living in a ground-floor apartment across the street from Second City, behind a Japanese restaurant. I remember the restaurant distinctly because Del's cat once stole a defrosting octopus from the back of the restaurant and dragged it into Del's living room. His apartment was literally squalor and roach infested. He was pretty used to this and really didn't mind it, as long as he had his books and electricity, which sometimes he borrowed from his upstairs neighbor by bringing down an extension cord. He would literally ask his neighbor if he could borrow a "cup of electricity." I was pretty appalled by his way of living. Del didn't seem to mind the roaches. He told me a story about an experience he had a couple of years earlier at The Goodman Theater. There was a party for Tennessee Williams. Many wealthy theater supporters were there to meet Mr. Williams. Robert Falls, the director of The Goodman Theater, brought a woman to meet Mr. Williams, who was standing alongside Del. Mr. Falls introduced the lady to Del. Del held out his hand to shake hands with the woman. As he took her hand, a roach crawled out from under Del's sleeve onto the woman's white glove. She screamed and ran away. Tennesse Williams looked at Del and said in a southern drawl, "Boy, I like your style."

While I felt that Del had a style all his own, I couldn't take his living situation. I was petrified to enter his apartment. I begged him to allow me to move him. His main concern over moving was that he was a book collector. He had books from floor to ceiling, wall to wall. Packing him up for a move would be like moving the Chicago Public Library. I promised him that he would not have to do a thing. I would have trustworthy students pack and move him. He asked me to

107

first try to have his place professionally cleaned. He wanted to see if we could avoid this most difficult move. If that didn't work, he promised he would give in. I hired an industrial cleaning service. I guess they were religious Christians because they came in and saw his altar, complete with swords and chalices, and ran out of the place in horror.

I found a place for Del directly across the street from where I was living — where I could keep an eye on him. We built him bookcases that were a book collector's dream. The place was beautiful and clean — best of all, no roaches. A few months after he moved out, the boiler at his previous apartment building exploded, and the building burned down. Del and his cats may have been killed if he hadn't moved, and certainly all of his books would have been destroyed. From then on, Del considered me his High Priestess.

CHAPTER 14:
The New Del

Now that Del was in a partnership with me, he had a clean apartment and clean clothes. I even convinced him to open a bank account despite his ridiculous fear that he might fall into the lake and get his bank book wet and never be able to retrieve his money. I had him eating and cooking in his new roach-free apartment and even got him a new television with a remote control and a comfortable study pillow to lean against while watching television in bed. I had thrown away his dilapidated black and white television along with its broken channel changer that Del had replaced with a wrench, which he used to change the channel. I had brought Del into the twentieth century. He now shared my theater company and had a manager (me) to make sure he got to auditions. I even convinced him to get a telephone. He had been afraid to have a phone in the past because if he watched the news and got mad at the President, he would call the White House and make threats. Then he would get arrested. I convinced him to call me first so that I could talk him out of calling and threatening the President. He gave in to me again. I was changing Del's life. In fact, I remember walking down the street with Del one day when he ran into an old friend. Del told his friend that he was no longer doing drugs and told him about everything going on in his life: his theater, his new acting career, me. The friend, who knew Del when Del was a junkie, looked amazed and said, "My God, Close, you've gone sane."

Del was considered a mad genius. I don't think he was mad — I think he was right. Don't get me wrong — he was a little strange, but much of that was for effect. I often felt like the aliens had dropped him off on Earth, and I was given the responsibility to care for him, and vice versa. One night, my parents took Del and me out for dinner. Since Del was so unique, my parents thought that I was afraid to tell them that I might be in love with Del. They decided to try to make things easier for us if that was the case. At dinner, my mother said, "Del, my husband and I want you to know that if you want to marry our daughter, we give you our blessing." Without missing a beat or even looking up from his wonton soup, Del replied, "No, thank you."

Del and I were family. Our relationship varied depending on what crisis we were facing. We were business partners, mother/son, father/daughter, mentor/student, best friends. Our theater does fine without him, but for me, it's not half as much fun.

An Insight into Del

My favorite part about watching Del's class was that he would always begin with a forty-five minute monolog about something he was reading that either affected him greatly or would be the impetus for the day's lesson. My favorite monolog was one about a book he had read by Norman Cousins:

Norman Cousins recently came out with a book called *Head First: The Biology of Hope*. It's about Holistic medicine and about the power of human mind and spirit to conquer disease. I'm for that. I'm for anything that puts the screws to the medical establishment. Yeah! Cousins's next book was called *The Anatomy of Adults* where he wrote about how he cured his leukemia by watching Buster Keaton movies, The Marx Brothers movies, and Laurel and Hardy movies on the hospital wall. He cured his leukemia through laughter. Ahoy there, Catholic Church. Are we paying attention here? I think we have some major miracle action on our hands. If the flickering images of dead comedians on a hospital wall can cure leukemia, isn't it about time we started talking about a little sainthood? St. Groucho, St. Ollie, the Blessed St. Gummo, the

Chapel of St. Laurel. I know, I know. The three stooges were Jewish and so were the Marx Brothers — but how about some ecclesiastical affirmative action here. So what if they're Jewish? St. Veronica was just a veil, for God's sake. Pope Joan was a woman. Oh, let Mother Theresa wait — she's not very funny anyway.

So, no matter what you think of Andrew Dice Clay ... he's cheap, he's sleezy, sexist, and dumb. But if he's out there getting laughs, he's doing God's work.

CHAPTER 15:
Del the Improviser

Del performed in many movies and plays and used his improvisational skills in his work. My favorite memory was when Del was in *Hamlet*, directed by Robert Falls at Wisdom Bridge Theater. Robert Falls had modernized this production of *Hamlet*. The actors wore suits and ties. There was a modern set with television screens everywhere so that the people throughout the kingdom could be watched — a comment on our day and age. Del played the role of Polonius. Del's vision of Polonius was a man who gave good advice; he just gave too much of it. He spoke very much like himself when he was in character. He became Polonius. Del was incredible in this role and even got better reviews than the star of the show, Aidan Quinn. In one scene, Del (or I should say Polonius) was giving orders to his assistant, Renaldo. Renaldo, played by J.J. Johnson, was supposed to take copious notes and, without even looking up, he was to light Del's cigarette. He was acting as the quintessential assistant — one who is there for every need. In this particular performance, J.J. stroked his lighter and thought he was lighting Del's cigarette. But the flame did not ignite. J.J. was directed to never look up or stop writing, and he assumed the cigarette was lit. Del improvised his next line: "*Oh, flick thy Bic once again, good Renaldo.*"

Del, a true improviser, was so smooth that this went over many heads. During the intermission I was in the washroom, and I heard one woman ask another, "Were all of Del Close's lines really in the play?"

Meet the Parents

Del was a book collector and had a book on every subject. He knew everything about anything. A visit to Del's apartment was always a fascinating experience. If we happened to discuss the Kabala, Del would begin his lecture as he walked to a bookcase and pulled out a book on the subject for me to take home. Of course, there would be three books I would have to read before the first one, and I would end up leaving Del's house armed with a stack of books. There was one night when we happened upon the subject of Masons. Del told me that he had joined the Masons but didn't make it to the highest level of Masonry. Apparently, the Masons were a mystical organization with strange rituals whereby the members would advance to becoming magicians at the highest spiritual level. He told me of secret rings, secret handshakes, and commitment ceremonies where members promise to never speak of what goes on in the meetings. It all seemed rather spooky, and I took home a few books that night.

About a month later, Del decided it was time to meet my parents. I was very nervous, to say the least. How silly of me! What could possibly go wrong? My parents were an affluent Jewish couple who owned three McDonald's franchises. Del was a former junkie, with track marks that covered his entire body, who hated organized religion and capitalism. He is the type of person who will say things to purposely shock people or take the opposing point of view just for the sake of conversation. He once defended Hitler in a conversation just because someone needed to take the opposing view. Del believed that if Hitler would have been admitted to art school, which is what he wanted in the first place, an art teacher could have channeled his energies in the right direction. "Just think of the great art we could have had today," said Del.

What could possibly go wrong? I was a nervous wreck.

We met at a steak house in Old Town, near Del's apartment. Del began showing his track marks to my mother pretty early on in the dinner. I guess he was testing her to see if she would run away screaming. But she was fascinated by his drug stories. My parents asked questions of Del regarding his opinions of comedians. "Do you like Jerry Lewis?" my mother asked. "No," Del replied tersely. "Why not?" she asked. Del slowly leaned forward and put his face up to my mother's face. "Because he's Jewish," Del said emphatically. I was worried. Disaster could be striking. I knew Del didn't hate Jews. He was just trying to see how my mother would react. My mom and dad both started laughing. They totally had Del's number. Del laughed too. I began to relax a bit more.

Suddenly, Del noticed a ring on my dad's hand. "Oh," said Del. "I see you're a Mason." My dad said that he was. "What degree are you?" Del asked. "Thirty-third degree," my dad replied. Del screamed with delight. "Charna, your father is a magician. He is more powerful than me!" Things were beginning to feel surreal. I looked at my dad and asked what Del was talking about. My dad just shrugged and winked at me as if to imply that Del was kidding. Del said, "He can't answer you, Charna. He is sworn to secrecy. You know that." Then, in a booming voice that was much like an imitation of Darth Vader, Del said, "I am your father!" I was scared and confused. I shot a glance at my father in the desperate hope that he would tell me it was all a joke. My father looked at me and said, "Well, you wanted him to like me."

CHAPTER 16:
Del and Chris Farley

For many years, Del and I were the only two teachers at i.O. The students started with me and then passed on to Del. I was always interested in seeing if my favorite students would become his favorites when they worked with him. I sat with Del on the first night of his new class. The students were always scared to move on from me, as I was considered a bit more nurturing than Del, to say the least. Del was a phenomenal teacher and would reveal the secrets of the universe to his actors. But if he didn't like you, watch out. One of the problems I had with Del was that sometimes, if he wanted to get rid of someone, he would whip out his checkbook and give the student his or her money back. That was his way of throwing them out. This used to upset me because he would do this when I wasn't there and there were many students who hadn't even paid for class yet. Here was Del giving two-hundred-dollar refunds to people who hadn't even paid us. Del would say, "It was worth it just to get rid of him."

But one night, there was someone I wanted Del to see. I waited to see what his opinion would be. Del watched a young man named Chris Farley play on-stage. After a few scenes, Del leaned over to me and said, "That's the next Belushi."

Years later, when we got the news that Chris was going to leave for New York to work for *Saturday Night Live*, Del and I took Chris out to a fine restaurant to celebrate and teach him some manners. As we waited for our table at the bar, Chris drank his beer so fast that it spilled down the side of his face. Del said, "Jesus Christ — no one is going to take it away from you. Slow down!" We told Chris we wanted to discuss his bad-boy behavior so that he could curb it in New

York. We were escorted to our table. Acting like a gentleman, Chris pulled out my chair for me. He noticed, when sliding in my chair, that the floor was highly waxed and extremely slippery. Chris whipped my chair — with me in it — across the room. Del went right on eating his bread and, once again, without missing a beat, said, "He's hopeless."

The week of Chris's first show on *SNL*, Del and I got a call from Chris. He was upset. *SNL* was making him dance without a shirt against Patrick Swayze. "They're making fun of the new fat boy," Chris whined. Del told him to dance the best he could and to pretend to be lighter than air. "Be the best you can be and don't let them turn you into a cliché," Del advised. Chris was phenomenal, and today that scene is one of their "best of" scenes.

The death of Chris Farley was very hard on both Del and me. Chris took part in my last book, and I feel I must take the opportunity to tell you how wonderful he was. i.O. lost two bright stars with the passing of Del Close and Chris Farley. I miss them both.

CHAPTER 17:
The Living Wake

Del called me in the late afternoon of March first. He was having hallucinations and seeing colors. In view of the hallucinations, he thought it might be a good idea for me to drive him to his class rather than him getting there on his own. I told him that if he was

Bill Murray, Charna Halpern, and Del Close at Del's living wake.

hallucinating, it might be an even better idea for me to take him to the hospital and cancel class for the day. He had no interest in going to the hospital. He said that he didn't mind the hallucinations at all and that the colors were quite lovely. He merely wanted a ride to class. I picked Del up and drove him to Illinois Masonic Hospital — with him kicking and screaming all the way. Despite the fact that Del was enjoying his hallucinations, I knew this meant that due to his emphysema, his brain was experiencing a lack of oxygen.

At the hospital, Del was given inhalation therapy, and he instantly looked better. He felt better, too, and thanked me for forcing him to go to the hospital. The emergency room doctor said that I saved his life. They wanted him to stay overnight for observation, and I would be allowed to pick him up in the morning.

The next morning, my phone rang at 5:00 a.m. It was a call from the hospital. They had to revive Del and intubate him. In layman's terms, that means they had to stick a tube down into his trachea, secure it, and attach it to a ventilator which blows oxygen into the lungs. I walked into the hospital room and saw Del strapped down to the bed. The reason they strap you down, for all you smokers out there, is that it's very painful, and you would want to tear the tube out of your throat. Del had tears streaming down his face. I knew Del well enough to know that this is not the way he wanted to die. I looked at him and cried. I said, "I remember you once telling me you didn't want this type of thing to happen to you." His eyes widened, and he emphatically nodded. "You want it taken out?" He nodded. I called the doctor to Del's room. The doctor said to Del, "You do understand that if we take this out, you aren't going to live." Del nodded. The doctor then said he would call inhalation therapy to come up to the room and take out the tube, and that we'd have about ten minutes to say our goodbyes. I kissed Del's forehead and told him how much fun he made my life. He motioned with his hand that he wanted a pen to write with. I got him a pen and paper. He managed to write while strapped down, laying flat on his back looking up at the ceiling. He wrote a note saying that I should get some *Truth in Comedy* books for him to sign because their value would go up. Here he was, trying to make me laugh in his last moments. Then he wrote a few other lines: "Death is not the enemy. Sorry kid — at least I got to see you one more time. Find yourself a young boyfriend like me."

The therapists came to the room. I was holding his hand and crying hysterically. This was it. I told him if there was any way for him to visit me from the afterlife that, by all means, he should come by. He nodded and squeezed my hand. They pulled out the tube. Suddenly, Del sat up and coughed. Then he stared screaming at the doctor, "How dare you rob me of my right to die with dignity? Get the hell out of here! How do I get some breakfast? I'm starving to death!" I stood there in shock. I felt like a car had run over me. I just went through a most emotional goodbye, and Del wanted breakfast.

Hours later, Del and I were visited for the first time by Dr. Julie Goldstein. Dr. Goldstein worked in Palliative Care. She came to see what Del's physical, psychological, and spiritual needs were at this time. She asked Del how, in his estimation, he thought he was (of course, she knew the answer. She just wanted to see if Del was aware of his dire situation). Del told her that he was dying. She asked him how soon he thought he would be dying, and he answered, "Any day now." In light of that, Dr. Goldstein asked if there was anything he would like to have happen in the next day or two. "I would like my sixty-fifth birthday party that I believe Charna was going to surprise me with. That would be the chance for me to say my goodbyes." Dr. Goldstein said that she could help make that happen. She and my brother-in-law, Dr. James Malow, gave me a tour of the hospital to let me choose the perfect "party" room for what was to be Del's living wake. There was a lovely big room in the basement of the hospital that I chose. Now it was time to invite the guests. The doctors told me the party had better be the next day if Del were to still be alive for it. I called Bill Murray. He told me that he would fly in immediately, and he'd make calls to other friends of Del's. He told me to order food from the finest caterers. And he wanted me to hire a sax player. He would cover the cost of the party. I told him we would be in a hospital, and I didn't think a sax player was a good idea. He insisted.

Dr. Goldstein and I returned to Del's room to tell him that the planning was in the works. Del then decided that he also wanted a Pagan ceremony with a High Priest and High Priestess dressed in full garb. He was a Pagan, and this would be equivalent to having his last rites. Dr. Goldstein and I went out into the hallway. "Where the hell am I going to get a High Priest and Priestess?" I asked. As I said these words, as if by magic, a social worker for the hospital happened to be passing by.

"Excuse me," he said. "I couldn't help overhearing. But I'm a High Priest, and I can get you a High Priestess. When do you need us?" Mystical things like that happened a lot where Del was involved, but that is for another book, as I'd hate for my readers to think I am just plain crazy. Everything was falling into place.

The next day over one hundred people filled the room. Bill Murray, Harold Ramis, and countless others from Del's Second City days were there, along with students and performers from i.O. as well as friends from other theaters in the City and two saxophone players (I followed Bill Murray's instructions to hire a sax player against my better judgment, but he didn't trust that I would, so he hired one just in case). I wheeled Del into the room. Bill and I flanked Del on each side as people stood in line to say goodbye to Del and thank him. I remember one woman said, "Del, I'm praying that you'll get better." Del growled at her, "I'm dying, damn it — just say goodbye." We gave speeches about Del and read telegrams from people like Peter Boyle and Howard Hessman and others who didn't have enough notice to fly in. Then the ritual began. A circle was formed around me and Del. Candles were lit, but the doctors made us blow them out instantly because of the danger of Del's oxygen equipment exploding. Del and I were each handed a white chocolate martini, and we toasted each other. Del was tiring, and it was time to take him back to his room. Bill and I wheeled him out of the party, and the room became silent. Everyone took their last look. On the way back to his room, Del said, "I guess I better die now, or a lot of people are going to be real disappointed."

CHAPTER 18:
A Profound Gift

Del died March 4th, 1999. A year prior to his death, I took Del to the doctor for a complete physical. It was then we were given the news that Del had emphysema and only a year to live. Del took the news better than I did. We decided it was time to get his personal affairs in order.

We went to a lawyer to make his Last Will and Testament. Del named me as the executor of his estate and will. I also had power of attorney in case anything happened in the hospital that made him unable to communicate his last wishes. As I said in the previous chapter, he was not one for life support.

It was my job to see that the few items he would leave to people were doled out according to his wishes. Larry Coven would get his first edition books, Howard Johnson would get his art collection. I got the rest of his estate which included his money, his magic wand, and a beautiful white cat named Cat Man Scruthers. But there was one more behest that would be my responsibility.

Del wanted his skull to be given to The Goodman Theater. He wanted his skull to be used in their next *Hamlet* production where he would play Yorick. Those of you who know your Shakespeare will remember the famous graveyard scene where Hamlet picks up the skull and says to his friend, "Alas, poor Yorick! I knew him, Horatio." That skull would be Del. Of course, Del was also willing to be a skull in other shows, perhaps a desert scene. He just wanted to keep working. It was now my job to pull this off.

It wasn't easy, but I kept my promise to Del. Months after Del's death, I held a ceremony in the Del Close Theater at i.O. In a crowded room full of press that would have put a presidential press conference to shame, I brought out Del's skull which rested on red velvet in a Lucite box. Tony Award winner Robert Falls met me on the stage to accept the bequest. To my surprise, Falls opened the box and picked up the skull. What happened next brought tears to my eyes and joy to my heart, as I knew it was exactly what Del would have wanted. Falls held out the skull in his right hand and spoke as the eloquent actor he is, "Alas, poor Del! I knew him, Horatio; a man of infinite jest." He continued on reciting the soliloquy. Del's wish had come true.

Today, Del's skull is at The Goodman Theater; his ashes are on a special altar that honors his life in The Del Close Theater — where he can affect the work. His thoughts and teachings are being spread all over the world.

i.O. is now a comedy empire with our theaters in Chicago and Los Angeles. And Del was right; we have created theater of the heart. When people cherish one another on-stage night after night, that can't help but fall off the stage and form incredible bonds between people. Those bonds turn into lasting friendships. i.O. has become a giant family that people stay a part of forever. Even those who go on to television and film still partake in performances here and teach opportunities to pass down the torch to the newer members of our family. The majority of the staff of *Late Night with Conan O'Brien, Saturday Night Live*, and *MADtv* consist of i.O. people who keep throwing down a line to hire others from here because they want to continue working with people who treat them the way we treat one another — like geniuses, poets, and artists. Del said that if we treated one another that way we had a better chance of becoming that on-stage. That was his way.

CHAPTER 19:
The Last Bastion
of the Counterculture

As Del mentioned in his opening interview, his ideas were based around the mindset of the 1960s. People were doing things in large groups, and peace and love were all the rage. Here at i.O. and at i.O. West, which is an extension of our Chicago Theater, we treat one another in a special way. As you have read, we take care of one another, we coach one another's teams, we play together, we inspire one another, and even help one another to get jobs.

Del always felt that with our work we were saving our corner of the world. We have taught that our improvisational theories should be applied to real life as well. Take care of one another. Do unto others as you would have them do unto you. Saying "yes" to one another's ideas is far more interesting than saying "no" and stopping any possibilities of something happening. We teach the concept of "yes" as a positive outlook to life. We teach the responsibility one has to trust others as well as being someone who can be trusted. We inspire students to be bold and fearless whenever they can.

i.O. has spawned theaters such as The Upright Citizens Brigade in New York and Los Angeles and inspired other theaters with our long-form work all over the world. *Truth in Comedy* is required reading in the theater departments on most college campuses across the nation. Even The American Embassy in Cyprus recognized the major importance of our work in agreement and hired me to work with the Greek and Turkish Cypriots in Cyprus in an effort to get them to agree and work together.

We will continue to send our message out to the world. We are a "theater of the heart." We continue to be progressive and cutting edge ... and we truly are the last bastion of the counterculture.

Life Is a Slow Harold

Our work is inspired by many scientific and mathematical principles of the physical world such as "the whole is greater than the sum of its parts." The mathematical theories of John Nash depicted in *A Beautiful Mind* dealt with each individual doing what is best for the group to succeed. Chaos theory deals with connections and the ordering of information out of chaos.

Del always said, *"Life is a slow Harold."* In your life you have probably experienced strange coincidences. But were they coincidences, or was the universe making connections all around you? The boy you beat up in grammar school just may end up being the brother of the girl you want to marry fifteen years later. The girl you cheat on in college may be the person interviewing you for that wonderful job opportunity later in life. I remember watching Bill Murray on *Saturday Night Live* in college, never dreaming that he would be helping me out with some of my most difficult moments later in life.

The greatest connection I ever experienced began in 1977. At that time I was teaching in a school for juvenile delinquent girls, and improvisation was the furthest thing from my mind. I had invited a young man over to my house for dinner. Thom was a musician who was also dabbling in acting. While I was preparing dinner, Thom played a tape recording for me. It was an interview he had just recorded with his teacher, who he found to be a most fascinating man. I listened while I cooked, but gave most of my attention to the great feast I was preparing. Thom told me he was inspired to write a song about this man's work. He went on and on about his fascination for this man, but I was truly much more interested in Thom than I was in his teacher. Thom's musical career took him on the road, and eventually we lost touch.

In 1985, a few years after Del and I began our partnership, we began to get a good deal of publicity in the newspapers. One day, I got a call from my long lost friend, Thom. He had read that I was Del's partner. He thought it was an amazing coincidence. I didn't know what he meant. He asked me if I remembered the night he came over for dinner and played that interview for me. I told him I remembered the evening well and had a vague recollection of the interview. He said that interview was with Del Close. "Who would have thought that years later you would be this man's partner?" said Thom.

Thom told me he had released an album which I immediately bought. The album contained a song that beautifully described the idea of being in the moment. I decided I wanted to use a stanza from that song for the opening in my book, *Truth in Comedy*. I called Thom and asked for permission. He knew right away which song I wanted to use. He said it was the song he talked about writing that night in my kitchen.

Pay attention to the connections in your life, and you, too, will see that life *is* a slow Harold.

> If you want to know where we went wrong
> You needn't look too far.
> For where we'll be and where we've been
> Is always where we are.
> And everything that comes your way
> Is something you once gave.
> Somebody feels the water
> Every time you make a wave.
> —Thom Bishop

 **i.O. Activities**

- Improvisational workshops for schools and theaters
- Corporate training and entertainment
- Shows tailored to special events
- Theatre training centers in Chicago and Los Angeles

For more details:
Website: www.ioimprov.com
E-mail: charna@ioimprov.com

i.O.
3541 Clark Street
Chicago, Illinois 60657
(773) 880-0199

i.O. West
6366 Hollywood Boulevard
Hollywood, California 90028
(323) 962-7560

Index

131

About the Author

Variety called her one of the top ten women to watch in entertainment. Mike Myers named her the Uta Hagen of Comedy. Charna Halpern, the co-creator of long-form improvisation with her partner, the late Del Close, has changed the face of improvisational comedy forever. Halpern and Close created their famous signature long-form piece, the Harold, a meta-game that "ate" short-form improvisation and became popular worldwide. Halpern and Close have been responsible for creating the talents and sensibilities of some of the biggest comedic stars in show business. Together and apart, their alumni include, John Belushi, Bill Murray, Gilda Radner, Mike Myers, Chris Farley, Tina Fey, Amy Poehler, Andy Dick, Andy Richter, Tim Meadows, Rachel Dratch, Horatio Sanz, Neil Flynn, Adam McKay, David Koechner, and many other illustrious cast members and writers of *Saturday Night Live, MADtv, Late Night with Conan O'Brien, The Daily Show*, and *The Colbert Report*. As director of i.O. in Chicago, (formerly ImprovOlympic) and i.O. West in Los Angeles, Halpern recently celebrated her 30th year in business. Under Halpern's guidance, i.O. is producing the next generation of artistic geniuses.

In addition to directing and teaching at i.O., Halpern travels the world teaching seminars in improvisation. She was hired by The American Embassy in Cyprus to teach her philosophy of agreement to the Greek and Turkish Cypriots in an effort to bridge their communication gap.

She is the author of *Truth in Comedy*, which is considered the bible for improvisation in the entertainment industry and is mandatory reading in theater departments on most college campuses.

She is not just a leader in the entertainment industry. She also has a reputation as the premier provider of corporate comedy and corporate training. Her workshops for corporations are customized to teach techniques in communication, team building, and creative thinking. Her methods of teaching agreement, building upon ideas, and turning a negative into a positive make for great sales tools and draw the parallels that exist between the improv world and the corporate work environment.

She recently returned to acting in a cameo role in a movie written and directed by Andy Dick, called *Danny Roane: First Time Director*.

She currently lives in Chicago with her two dogs, Chief and Mia, and travels back and forth to her theater in L.A.

Order Form

Meriwether Publishing Ltd.
PO Box 7710
Colorado Springs, CO 80933-7710
Phone: 800-937-5297 Fax: 719-594-9916
Website: www.meriwether.com

Please send me the following books:

_____ **Art by Committee (book and DVD)** $22.95
#BK-B284
by Charna Halpern
A guide to advanced improvisation

_____ **Truth in Comedy #BK-B164** $17.95
by Charna Halpern, Del Close and Kim "Howard" Johnson
The manual of improvisation

_____ **112 Acting Games #BK-B277** $19.95
edited by Gavin Levy
A comprehensive workbook of theatre games

_____ **Improv Ideas #BK-B283** $24.95
by Justine Jones and Mary Ann Kelley
A book of games and lists

_____ **275 Acting Games: Connected #BK-B314** $19.95
by Gavin Levy
A comprehensive workbook of theatre games for developing acting skills

_____ **The Ultimate Improv Book #BK-B248** $17.95
by Edward J. Nevraumont, Nicholas P. Hanson and Kurt Smeaton
A complete guide to comedy improvisation

_____ **Group Improvisation #BK-B259** $16.95
by Peter Gwinn with additional material by Charna Halpern
The manual of ensemble improve games

These and other fine Meriwether Publishing books are available at your local bookstore or direct from the publisher. Prices subject to change without notice. Check our website or call for current prices.

Name: _____ email:_____

Organization name: _____

Address: _____

City: _____ State: _____

Zip: _____ Phone: _____

❑ **Check enclosed**

❑ **Visa / MasterCard / Discover / Am. Express #** _____

Signature: _____ Expiration date: _____ / _____ CVV code: _____
(required for credit card orders)

Colorado residents: Please add 3% sales tax.
Shipping: Include $3.95 for the first book and 75¢ for each additional book ordered.

❑ *Please send me a copy of your complete catalog of books and plays.*

About the *Art by Committee* DVD

The DVD for *Art by Committee* contains performances
by the following improv groups:
Upright Citizen's Brigade
The Armando Diaz Theatrical Experience and Hootenanny
Beer Shark Mice
The Reckoning
Peter Hulne

The DVD also contains interviews with the
following improv artists:
Adam McKay
Amy Poehler
Andy Dick
Rachel Dratch
Stephnie Weir
Tim Meadows
Tina Fey